Sunwind

Sunwind

CLINTON F. LARSON

Edited and with an introduction by
David L. Evans

GENEVA STEEL CORPORATION

To the pioneers of the mind and spirit at Geneva,
who make things possible

And to the Celtic people, who Christianized Europe

I am grateful for my colleagues and friends,
and for the editorial work of
Wayne Taylor and Miriam Pierce.

ISBN 0-916095-34-7
Geneva Steel Corporation, Orem, Utah

Cover Photograph: Wm. Floyd Holdman
Printed in the United States of America

Deirdre

Forever the cup of Christ and Excalibur,
That shaped our prayer for Erin. Goodbye!
Goodbye, Erin!

Sing of evening, the Lotus whispers,
Sing of midnight; sing of the breeze
That makes blossoms speak of their desire,
Calming into silence, drifting into sleep,
Away from stem, but held and held in fire,
Faith's fire that must weep as falls
Of water weep at evening, sunset's falls
Of light across them burning in.
The flame of sun makes the morning come!
Oh, weep for morning, morning's ushering,
And sing . . .

—from my poetry drama Deirdre and Naisi

Contents

Introduction: By Way of an Invitation

"Say, why not turn off the tube for a while—or stay home from the game this evening—and instead read a poem or two?" Most Americans nowadays are likely to react to such an invitation much as the boll weevil in the Pogo comic strip reacted to Churchy LaFemme when the latter asked him if he would like to hear "a poem I just wrote": "No thanks, I read one in nineteen ought twenty-two." But I am repeating the invitation to you to spend at least a few moments and, I hope, quite a bit longer, reading not just any few poems but quite specifically a few poems from this collection by Clinton F. Larson, one of the true phenomena of Utah culture.

I don't want to harangue anyone about the abstract values of poetry, but I would like to comment on a few of the qualities of Clinton's poems, especially his simultaneous appeal to eye and mind. In a sense, Clinton is a painter who picked up a notebook and the dictionary instead of canvas and a box of oils. Robert Browning described extremely well the appeal of the artist (he was speaking of a painter, but what he said applies equally well to the poet) when he allowed his character Fra Lippo Lippi to explain,

> we're made so that we love
> First when we see them painted, things we have passed
> Perhaps a hundred times nor cared to see. . . .
> God uses us to help each other so,
> Lending our minds out.

Certainly, in these poems Clinton lends out his eyesight and his insight, so that we may *see* in both meanings of the word.

A glance through the book will, I hope, reveal the pattern I have tried to follow in organizing the poems. The first group includes subjects everyone is acquainted with, and the titles emphasize this: "Granddaughter," "First Grader," "Sleeping in Church." Or the subject may be a person Clinton has known and who represents a type or a situation we have all experienced in one way or another: "Brooke Porter, a Lover of Pets," "To a Dying Girl," "Jesse." In all these early poems we find Clinton speaking of people we may not have known in person but come to *feel* we know now. And we can see the people vividly with our imagination's eye: the grandchild spilling oatmeal and looking guiltily up, then murmuring "Amen" as an innocent's form of penance; the small child gripping her father's finger for reassurance as she approaches the chapel on Sunday morning; Brooke Porter, bringing home every stray kitten she finds; the eighty-five-year-old woman "Sleeping in Church"; the "Nearly Forsaken" young relative, crying in a cousin's closet "in the loss of the one whose being was her being." The appeal to the eye is strong, but even stronger is the appeal to the mind, as we share the awareness of the grandparents' need for loving patience; the father's recognition of all the radiance his shy daughter adds to Sunday and the world; Brooke's embryonic motherhood which motivates her assembling the stray animals of the world; the beauty and inner sincerity illustrated by the octogenarian woman's sleeping in the arms of Jesus; the universal cry for compassion welling out of the forsaken child, to be met only with "That child needs a whipping."

The second group includes poems about places we may know personally or at least know about: Cascade Springs, the Tetons, the nostalgic oldtime musical theatre in Jackson Hole, Palm Beach, Camino Real, the "White Water" of a wild river, even the Utah valleys, as they are represented in "Homeland" and "Joseph Smith's Vision." Closely related are the next poems, works in which we move a little farther from the people we know to activities we all share: class reunions, delighting in the aroma and taste of freshly baked "Finely-textured Bread," meditating on lady bugs or commiserating at the death of a friend's favorite cat, watching the children embark on a Halloween adventure in, not the welfare but the "Malfare of Late October," or "Cubing Dowd with a Cold." Whether sharing actual places or general activities, we find the poet again lending his eyesight and insight to us.

The next group of poems are alike in sharing widely different aspects of one of the truly universal subjects, love. Clinton is not writing the story of one specific couple; he deals instead with the universals of love as they become manifest within all of us. From the "First Encounter" through the complication and casualties to the "Wedding Morn" and final memories, he recounts the many subtle experiences and awarenesses of all people. This section is fulfilled by the story of one specific couple, the story of "Guy Coleman, the Singer of Midway" and his beloved Teresa.

Poems in the next main group move out to another circumference: to the modern world—the types of people and the activities which characterize our national life. Here we find "Fred Astaire," "Morrey the Fox," the "great pundits" of the sports page, the self-important moguls of the universities and of the television world. A special section here focuses on the terrors which accompany modern technology: the power of machines like the "Machine Press," always waiting for the innocent blunder of the operator, the moment of inattention; the ever-present destructiveness of the automobile "Ascending from a Divider" or, in a head-on crash, snuffing life out horrifically in "Seven-tenths of a Second" or the airplane, in an "Emergency Landing" converting the triumph of returning to earth without a flaming, gigantic crash into the tragedy which results from a lesser crash caused by "downing into a fence."

Still part of the visual world we know are the events

chronicled from a creative point of view in the next two small
groups of poems: the historical insights from the Civil War and
World War II, from the Twentieth Maine Regiment to the Viet-
nam War Memorial. Then from these we move to Egyptian history, with Ramses II serving as both entry and exit.

Readers already familiar with Clinton's poetry will feel at
home in the next group: poems which begin with a clearcut
image or pattern of images but which quickly change in time
or place, and then move to a series of impressions in which the
visual image gives way as the center of the poem and a mental
response becomes the focus. The simplicity and everyday quality of the poems early in this volume are replaced by an esthetic
awareness of the experience of a larger life; the intellectual
quality becomes stronger. Comparisons of different cultures
become significant, and allusions serve a deeper function. The
lakeshore in the poem of that name is not the shore of a specific lake which we appreciate for its local color; it is a lake of
the archetypal imagination, a subjective locale appropriate to
the poet as he "move[s] upon the light and stand[s] in the
tours / Of spirit"; a place where the reader can accompany the
poet as he moves "into the light / That fins the air with lustre
that the spirit stores."

One of Clinton's favorite types of subject matter for such a
treatment is religion. The religious element becomes increas-
ingly stronger in these poems until we find ourselves in "Christ
the Magician," "Theology," "The Other Mary," and "Resurrection." Perhaps the type of subject in which he most distin-
guishes himself as a poet of the mind, concerned with the
religious implications of all philosophical and scientific
thought, includes the poems in which he begins with images
viewed from the vantage point of the scientific investigator, then
looks for the timeless, archetypal human elements within the
images, and at the end harmonizes these complex elements

with a spiritual accommodation to the world. "Glacier" and "Mountains," for instance, may sound at first like titles to introduce simple if effective images from a wilderness setting, but instead they lead us through science to the visions of the religious mind. This quest is given voice in "Glacier," for example, when the poet avers, "The lost azimuth bequeaths the dark wisp / Of its eternity and the Word in the lisp / Of this geology," and the mountains "in their majesty are a trait / Of sun, a promise of the vale of amethyst / Amid the stars, a remnant of the primal / Energy, O Alpha, in a vagary of the sunstream / Will." An interesting comparison can be made if one reads first "Tetons," a poem in which the actual mountains retain their individuality, and then "Mountains," in which the philosophical and religious intensity wrench the setting out of the physical into a purely intellectual setting.

By now it should be obvious that my invitation to you to look more widely and more deeply into this book is based on a recognition that here is a banquet table spread with victuals for every taste. For those who want to get more deeply acquainted vicariously with people, places, and situations which they already know, there are poems galore. For those who want to delve below the surface (those who will say with Melville, "I love any fish that dives"), there are plenty of works here with lower layers well worth the plunge. For those who want challenges simultaneously to the mind, the sensibility, and the soul, there are poems of universal significance combining science, philosophy, and religion. And for the reader who wants rather the poetic charms for the ear, eye, and other senses, who respects poetic form for its own sake, here is a plenteous feast. If I have stressed above, Clinton's appeal to sight and to the mind, let no one assume that he lacks literary craft or is insensitive to the sounds and associations of words. Let anyone who questions his skill read, for example, "To a Dying Girl." As a bonus, there is the wit which invests so many of the verses, whether it takes the form of wordplay (often in the titles as well as in the poems themselves), gentle humor, or biting satire, particularly in his portraits of modern academic or materialistic types.

At first one may feel it a trifle unexpected that such a poetic feast should be sponsored by a steel factory. The traditional concepts of the poet and the American steel mills seem rather inharmonious. I must confess that I was a bit surprised myself when Clinton first told me of this partnership. The administration of Geneva Steel is indeed to be commended for recognizing the worth of Clinton's poetry and then making it available to many readers. A few parallels between Geneva and the poet do present themselves: both are part of the Central Utah scene; both are associated with the valley, the mountains, and the people who live here; and both have had their share of critics as well as supporters among those people. But another parallel suggests itself. Allow me to shift the figure of the feast to another type of metaphor. Like the maker of steel, the poet mines his materials from deep within, then brings a variety of resources together so that they can be fused and the dross removed. A shower of sparks attends the one process literally, the other figuratively. And if all is done right, the finished product is strong, bright, and capable of enduring.

I believe that the process *has* been "done right" in the poems in this volume. That is why I repeat my invitation: Take a few minutes away from the TV set or other diversions you are about to pursue and try some of the poems in this book—even if, like Pogo's boll weevil, you have read one as recently as nineteen ought twenty-two. If you find the first few to your taste, read on. I hope you will accept my invitation, not because of what it will do for me or Clinton, but what it may do for you.

—David L. Evans

Sunwind

Granddaughter

Next to tears for the supposed naughtiness
Of tipping oatmeal from her pastel bowl
And spilling milk under our haughtiness,
She displays the repentance of her soul

Over there. Her gaze is tenuous with sorrow
As she looks at the world, hoping for the best,
Arms folded to gather herself for the harrow
Of scolding. "Amen," she says in a tentative test

Of our love, grace over, but willing to pray.
I saw that the lip of her tray had tipped her bowl,
She not knowing why her oatmeal in disarray
Was so, but feeling the sackcloth of her role.

And there stand I as well with her as anywhere,
Marvelling how to keep some order at hand,
Displaying my hope glossily to keep fair
Days of charity flowing like hourglass sand.

First Grader

She can draw, or maneuver pieces of a puzzle
(Is it jigsaw, tinker, rubric?), and so confound
Adults into an amazement through which, so profound,
She cleverly saunters, neatly original, to nuzzle
Up to Merlin in a primer book, though never to muzzle
Any ilk of storyteller. Her feeling surely as sound
As thinking, she considers backyard denizens bound
By duties of affection, including birds and chuzzle-
Wits. Neatly riding whatever crest (joy, bluegrass,
Wind), she appoints discourse with dayspring blue,
Lifting forward into fairest reasoning to surpass
Our logic, offering violets to affluent us to sue
For favors for various waifs. I say, in sobriety,
That she will ever be president of a relief society.

Christopher in Church

My mommy's speaking in this church.
    She's left me with a relative,
    My father. So I use an expletive
To get attention and begin to search

For my train. It's in Mommy's purse.
    Down the aisle I go, "Choo! Choo!"
    And up stairs on my knees to view
So many folks facing me. I rehearse,

"Choo! Choo!" grab her dress and legs,
    And look at them below the small talk
    Drone. "Bzz!" I drag my chalk
Across the carpet as she begs

Me not to, kneeling down. Escaping,
    I become a tall giraffe swaying
    On seats or a gray coyote baying
To the choir, and then, draping

Myself over a bench, I hoot and rail
    As she holds me near, blushing.
    But I break loose, pell mell rushing
To the pipe organ, where I sail

Into the scrim, tumble over feet,
    Tromp the keys, drifting sand,
    And, delving for a rubber band,
Flip it at a deacon. I repeat

My repertoire as the choir of hoods
    Scatters. I wish I had my Tommy
    Gun, with pellets. Come on, Mommy.
Let's lock horns and trumpet in the woods.

Susan at Three

Because it dangled at my side, the nearest
Finger to her, and sized just right, and, lo,
Verily for her to grab so firmly, wisely so,
She did it for Sunday, for me to guide her lest
She trip through it on her way before her rest
Against my arm during Sunday School, to flow
Through lessons of it smiling to hear, to slow
The meaning of Sunday's sound, to know how best
To act, to be the Sue she was, and is. Her radiance
Abounded at the door as she skipped and settled
Into such decorum. But it must learn from her
How to turn the churchly order, I aver,
So well to joy as it should be, unnettled
So as not to disturb her, or me, tossing
Her golden hair to right and left, embossing
Sunlight, making it more golden everywhere.

Brooke Porter, A Lover of Pets

She would pronounce "two" to make it seem an identical rime with "yew," as in "English Yew," and one would dote on it as if to think that she was a real aficionado of homey effects. Well, she was, certainly, a friend of every denizen of nursery rimes, and then some, whistling and humming her way through her studies.

Kitties and teddy bears provided her province. Teddy bears were in a half-circle on her bed. One had "M and M" written across it. But she was always on the prowl for a real, furry kitty.

Often she would see one, or a litter, and come home, wide-eyed, and ingenious, to announce that it was "kewt," and look up pleadingly for corroboration. We said that it must be, if she said so.

"Can I have it?" she asked.

Our tenuous "uh-uh" was a last resort of opinion. How could we say "yes"?

"There are two," she said.

If we said yes to that, we mused, the cute, cuddly animals of the world would line up behind her, waiting for the warmth of her motherhood.

Ballet

The effortless lift, as if she is nothing
But silk and pointed toes, and her hair,
Fallen back in the wind, rustles, sere
In the light, but flowingly gold. Something
Stirs. It is music from the bowstring
Of great Orion, who loosed the bright, rare
Starlight quivering, and then, lowly, the flare
Of the glancing vision and belling stinging
Across the intervening hush of an audience
Caught up in a reprise of the first invention.
What is it but glissando and the retention
Of pearling form that surpasses the science
Of metric gravity? It is a touch into nothing
That created the spheres silver, the silvery mothing
Of shaken dew, and elision suddenly rousing
Into glimmer and gold.

Nearly Forsaken

The decision arose from logic and necessity.
She was received by an aunt's daughter to tend,
And she began to cry against the knee of the one
Who had to leave for just a time. "I have to,
Honey," reverberated in her listening before
It happened, disquieting her like a sadness
That it should never happen. "Please don't go!"
She cried, emptying her early soul at the door
Into the stillness. So she stood at the door,
Lost, as the one who had kept her waved farewell.
Inconsolable, she remained in distances from home,
Away from comfort and comforting. The doll
Of celluloid, jacks for the doorstep, patent
Leather shoes with straps, the apple tree back
Of the sleeping porch, and the playhouse Father
Had built, now gone into the memory of memory.
Now was ravaged, and nothing remained for her
In the loss of the one whose being was her being:
Security of home, and comfort, and her bed, secure
In herself, a place to be. She cried for the one
Who had gone for another's need. She found the edge
Of her hand and gripped it to keep it against her,
Against her side, and looked up, not seeing
For tears. And so the cousin, at a loss
About what to do, gave her a place in a closet
To forget, or to quiet the child, perhaps to let
Her turn her attention to a toy inside to staunch
Her tears. But there is a remorse in sorrow

Beyond recall as utter loss beyond the scape
Of vision, that is its own. She ran her fingers
Against a hem that she could not feel or sense,
Against the soles of her shoes that were not there,
Against the closet door that was hard as rock
And cold as the shades of winter, crying, crying
For the one who was gone, to come, to return, to whisper
To her, perhaps consoling, forever forgiving,
To keep her again. Outside, the voice came again,
"That child needs a whipping, she carries on so.
Maybe we could put her outside, or in the garage."
And failing into another emergency, it diminished
Into a softer stridence. But in the closet
The girl cried into the welling distances of loss,
For anything of home, or its memory, even something
To touch. But her soft fingers slipped away,
Ice against the sense of ice, the loss remaining
As memory only, memory gone, identity gone
In a closet like perpetual home, the walls,
The door, and the linen in a boundless emptiness.

Sleeping in Church

Lovely. Lovely. She brought her rickety bones
And her belief to church, and now she sleeps.
Hardly in the arms of Morpheus, who weeps
In envy of her peace, she nods as she atones
For every ill she thought of, amid the knowns
And unknowns of this life. A low moan seeps
From chief authority that she abridges and defeats
His charismatic rule, though he busily hones
The edge of Calvinism, grim and erstwhile,
Mulling doctrine. But Sunday is a day
Of rest, as she knows it. Who would defile
Such peace? Not I. The church is hers, a way
To house the inner light and the inner sight
Of God it proffers, not the whittling spite
Against her Christian will. Oh, lovely, lovely she,
Aging at eighty-five in the arms of her creator!

To a Dying Girl

How quickly must she go?
She calls dark swans from mirrors everywhere:
From halls and porticos, from pools of air.
How quickly must she know?
They wander through the fathoms of her eye,
Waning southerly until their cry
Is gone where she must go.
How quickly does the cloudfire streak the sky,
Tremble on the peaks, then cool and die?
She moves like evening into night,
Forgetful as the swans forget their flight
Or spring the fragile snow,
So quickly she must go.

Jesse

We stumbled up the stairs, onto the back porch,
Where Jesse's father kept his hunting gear,
His shotgun leaning against a porch screen
That puffed a mist of dust when touched or rubbed.
So Jesse said, "Look out. The step is loose."
We went in, asking his mother, Leah, for time
To ride out to the lake. With her assent,
We left, grazing the evening with whispering,
And threw blankets over the horses whose reins
We left slack to the ground. We steadied them
And jumped up easily, jostling and settling
Where best to ride. Then off into the evening,
Wresting from the near air intimacy and warmth
Of summer. And we rode down the even lane,
Grass and darkness to either side, the katydids
Sounding over the rhythm of the horses we kept
In the surer way, peering somberly as we went.
Jesse felt the defection from day and the tug
Of seeming to have lost it so early, after play.
He said: "The day was short enough; evening
Brings the sound of water up the shining sand.
Let's see, tonight, how high the dark lakewater
Must rise to touch the willows on the shore
Where the inlet keeps its secrecy." I nodded,
Softly yielding to the restraint of solemnity,
Reaching forward to the mane for firm balance.
I said, "A rift of light rests forward here.
Let's follow it." And he replied, "I find
The sallow world at the far edge of my hand,

And the restless rainwind veers across the lake.
I left my father and mother in the livingroom
Wondering why I leave them, even with you.
Questions glanced across their faces like shadows
Of boughs lifting in the breeze of evening.
I should return. But the leafing air grazes
My loneliness. Out there, where the evening
Fails, stars appear in the dark paling sky
Like memory returning." And we rode silently
As I heard the grasses against the hooves,
Near the lake. And I saw the lancet dark
Invade the gloss of water and the rippling light.
I looked at him askance and saw his eyes
And the gild of water draw a shining sleep
Into them. And as we returned, he softly rehearsed
The gentle inflections of light he knew. He said,
"I know the prince that stands beyond the air."
And afterwards, when in England I caught news
Of him in the random vision of words in print,
Newsprint fragile and yellowing as it seemed
To slip and fall from an envelope, I knew
He stumbled from step to porch, near the screen,
And jarred the bluesteel set of hammer and shank
That his father had left for his quick return.
And at once I felt the slow gait of the horses
Near the lake, where the lights of evening ease
And whisper into being beyond the gloss of day.

Waiting for a Soldier, 1917

The dull daguerrotype holds her image
As if on weave of linen. Light grazes
Her surface, whose immediate glow amazes
Our memory. She was young before the rage
Of contravening hate in the fiery cage
Of war, when restitution began in phases
On the kaiser's front among mounds and mazes
Of Verdun, the continuity. Hail, gut of sage
And soldier in a wiry violin, excrescent
And warbling gas in its venue, chlorine
Nestling in a lung that sogs in a tureen
Of skull, whose strewn mind, recent
In its occupancy, is green in the rush
Of death like proud flesh, the intaglio.

Cascade Springs

At the circumventing elevation of meadow-stirring stars,
Mallow lilies, leaves in water, and the flow of springs,
I wait. The subterranean whisper of water brings
The soul to bear the radiances of day in the spars
Of glimmering dawn. The angling dayspring chars
Gray into silver, brown into faery gold, sand of things
Helter-skelter in butternut leaves as bistre stings
Them up to be noticed as nearby flowering. The cars
Of morning are swatches of color imbuing an incline,
As if one could walk there to the sun. I recline
In the meadow grass, in warming sun, over the scars
Of moonmist summer. Children have seen this sign
And keep its wonder, tossing the morning and coloring jars
Of their containment in kindergarten classes to define
Their natures in nature, in such very lucid weather.

Coal Towns

India grey, smoke grey, pearl grey, nigre
Of pallor. The street rises luminously
Into dawn, and houses keep themselves faring well,
Each for its comfort echoing the fathering bell
Of morning to make them all and always deliciously
New to day. This is Merthyr Tydfil overcoming
Listlessness, no matter what it yearly puts away,
Souls of coalmen overbending town and parish
After perishing. From the cleft of canyon,
Time zones west, cars of mounded coal
Move to the hearths of Geneva, furnaces
Of pearling fire, strontium and saffron
Billowing into stacks and drifting grey
Where yardlights illumine dark
Under the clerestory drift of noon.

Homeland

Homeland, your vast scape, in a sea of light,
Smooths into the paradisal green of uplands
And the topaz fields of desert. Curves of light
Are languid over surfaces: near blue, far purple.
Silver along the floors of sand, sage green
Over slopes, and silver in vestments of morning,
Unknowing, but ready for the flourish of glory.
It may come as the petal of region lifts away,
Or as a gust billows in the sage, or as a caress
Of light over the still air, or as the long lake
Of salt trembling away like a line of silver:
The hues are sharp and clean, and the fierce eagle
Planes over the landward expanse, alert as a gleam
Of air.

Joseph Smith's Vision

Joseph, the ache
Of your vision is with us
and must be fulfilled.
I have looked into your eyes
And have seen the far horizons of the West,
The wagons and the prairies white and golden
Under a summer day. I have seen the cleavage
Of land from the mountains
Where the gulls
Ride above a silver sea and the sky
Like a veil hangs over a great valley,
Where the people may gather, where
The mountains decline with the sun.
In the west the valley lies: the great blue peaks
Rise in the haze where the wagons go; where we go
The land is like the palm of God.

Brigham Young's Challenge

Palm Beach

Step down. Repose, the gentle decline to the sea,
Is the still tumult of sand that becomes the meridian
Vanishing north and south, smooth as an obsidian
Mirror. It is sand smoothing again to be
The cool surface of impenetrable hours that fall
Downwind, westerly, the soft Floridian
Topaz in your eyes. It is October, and the carnelian
Lotus floats on the sea and bequeaths itself in the lea
Of morning, evening failing the surrogate harlequin
Topaz of light of porticos. I suggest a retreat
And music in a hideaway where waiters, replete
With offerings, hesitate to serve. You are a mannequin
So perfectly adorned that I too must hesitate
To know propriety. But must one exacerbate
Love to love and let love be as natural
As experience?

Camino Real

The file of clouds abrades the crescent blue.
And the urgent morning grows clearer, even fair
With the prize of prisms dusting where
Greening of ochre rises from ochre to renew
Another yesterday. What can one do
To sense the matching light that keeps the stir
For newest color? As it were
Is memory lidded with the bistre burr
Of gold, a medallion burst of sun that I drew
From sleep. Imagine that whatever may occur,
The file of ochre, or sierra, or the whirr
Of wings, or whatever color may ensue
As emblem, in hue or golden haze, will wear
A frock or mantle nearest you that glows as evidence.

Tetons

Stacked largely clear before the eyes,
Sierra too brazen for common belief,
They were and are stone windreef,
Cirque and light, the shadowed size

Of passing cloud, O will of noon
To charge the air close by to revise
Flow of vision as we devise
The mind to remember the rune

Of being. Vale and wind, pines
Against gray, water an inkling
Of blue, and there a ravine tinkling
Rain in trees as dark defines

The sound of evening where moraine
Mounds from lake and fields of larkspur,
Willows wavering, marsh and lure
Of inlet, shore, and the hovering rain.

Musical Theatre in Jackson Hole

At the central park where horns embellish an arcade,
You can see the silver spur, the saddlery, and the bank
As on the ball of your foot you manage to yank
Yourself around. Your horse ambles too as you parade
Under a balustrade to sing of Ramona as you invade
The commercial ambiance. You huckster too, blank
As Personality. Upstairs, a garter is pink. You flank
An usher and push in, as you resent yourself and abrade
Your insubordinate horse, who becomes as vain
As you thought he was in the stable. You sit with him
On the first row, showing your teeth. The lights dim,
And the production begins like the lights of a train
Down a track. Then you brace yourself as your hackles
Rise illustriously, only slightly repressed by shackles
That reach up to your dander.

The City of Joseph, 1980

What is this soft array of leaves and light
But morning? The sky opens with the wind
That caps the upper branches like spume,
Whiteness over them sweeping mist that rises
From meadows. And now what is the array of light
As one looks down upon the city's scape
Of buildings? The places where Joseph came
To find his Zion are in the spell of prophecy,
The sound of vision, and moments of his certainty.
One could believe that trees and buildings might be
Alike if through half-closed eyes the gathering
Of overcast and light might yield green and ochre
Steadily as earth's visions appear around them
And surely as the events of time that brought
The few together in a home to harvest
Centuries of tendency. What tendencies hover
In a prophecy or dream? The path in a glade
May be the boulevard, and a holy place
May be the place of sacrament, where visions
Come and elide distinctions that diminish
The prospect of meaning. The holy place may be
A room, a shelter of trees, a lake where white
Flickers through a scape of gray and green,
As if moraine where suddenly the crest of land
Keeps the air calm or fleeting. Joseph,
The few began the order of the Son of God,
Elijah and Melchizedek of Salem near at hand,
The plates of gold before them in whose radiance
The time became a sepulchre, language

The spirit before them, fluid in its power,
The dust of gold from ages of Teotihuacan
And the sunburst on a floor receiving sun
And prophecy from the angels of the gold
And turquoise. Canyons open, glistening
Red and green, cliffs and mesas in a curve away,
The distant mists of glory azure-lidded
And hidden in the vision of an ancient city,
Zarahemla, where towers held the words
That Nephi rendered on India gold. O city,
Your subtle glades of light, your boulevards
Open outward always as if to receive
The steady radiance of sun and sunburst,
Of Arcturus or Orion, Sun, and Aldebaran
Shimmering like leaves. I saw, not long ago,
A little girl close the door of her home in Nauvoo
And go to flowers she had planted by a spring.
The yellow and auburn of her dress, the white knots
In her braided hair, her eyes that kept their blue,
Despite the array they saw, seemed kept in light
In the afternoon. Her mother quietly followed her
To the fence and stood there watching: "Margaret,
You must leave them now. Put those in your hands
Aside and come with me." "Where, Mother?"
She asked, slowly turning. "We must leave
This home and find our way across the prairie
West." "Just across the river?" "Westward
Still, to a place called Laramie, and farther on,
Beyond the rising slope, to peaks and canyons
I have never seen." "Why?" she asked as soon
As she could lay her flowers beside the ones
That remained near the fence. "Because we believe."

"Mother, why do we believe as we do?" "Joseph
   Came and talked to us about a harvesting."
"But Joseph is gone." "We believe as he believed.
   Come. We must leave Nauvoo, and home, and find
   Our way to Laramie." Later, on the prairie,
   The girl and her mother walked together, the wagon
   Ahead jostling through grass. Beyond, shadows
   Of clouds spilled over a butte, and the red
   Of its stone seemed leaden in hollow distances.
"Why do we believe as we do?" The girl dangled
   A doll by the arm as she walked, believing
   The prophecy of the city west in the mountains,
   If not Zarahemla, Deseret, in the span
   Of landfall east of the Sierra Nevada range
   And the lake nearer still. I have heard
   The whisper of the wagon wheels in the canyons,
   The prophecy of wind over prairies, the cry
   Of hosanna in the gray cirques of vision:
   Home, the city is home, the slope of loam
   And moraine against the cliffs, the twinkling
   Of towns as the evening comes to Zion.
   Time elides antiquity and the nearby years.
   Margaret came with her doll in her arms,
   Believing, and her great, great grandchildren
   Gather their children around to tell how she
   Came to the valley, stood on a hill to the east,
   And cried her devotion.

White Water

White spire of winds, they wrest you white, rushing
Before the sea of the lake at its severance
Of shores. Snow thins down the long slope
Of its wisping. Then the rush, the lift, the bustling
Of the invisible across old silver rustling
With skiff and sail dodging into the valence
Of the morning. Sails mount this veering silence
Like vanes and leap before they fall, hustling
Far to meet the silver rising from the vales
Of water sunmetal black, or blue if lightened
From the whip of silver dulling and rimming
The slopes from whence it came. The wind of sails
Rails before the sound of lashing and booming into the flare
That brightens in upon our knowing the shire and share
Of the vaster sea.

Fiftieth High School Reunion

Aye, at the entrance and down a ramp to park
Underground, and then to emerge into the foyer
Resplendent for Review. Thus, like a voyeur,
I lilt among and between to find the shark
Of protocol who will know enough to cark
About morale and who knows a few: lawyer,
Executor, buddy, stuffed shirt, and Tom Sawyer
Of the neighborhood I knew who made his mark
In kilts, now sporting floosie. The faces
Mean nothing, having drawn and aged anonymously,
But I peer at names and, quite tenuously,
At ancient photos from yearbook, finding traces
Of remembrance there! and there! "Hello, Don,
Is it you at this hurrah? Or are you really Sean
O'Casey, playwright with an Anglo-Irish glint?
I shall address you from the forlorn past,
When we were giddy saints of youthful caste,
Callow in our dolor, fishing forth for a hint
Of what to do with living largely before the stint
Of coming war, we who made it through, still fast
Friends, expansive at the waist and, at last,
Successful!" I do not doubt, of course, the mint
Of this production, having risen through the ranks
To station wiser, sheen of eye, milling affluence
Into bread, and tossing it upon the confluence
Of all society as a moiety of valor. The pranks
Of image that time imposes must fail thereby
And must vanish into gleam like the finesse whereby
We must and do remember!

Finely-Textured Bread

Whatever the recipe, which may include the leaven
Of manna and certainly gluten, it glows in tins,
And one is therefore wont to cancel all sins
With a penitence of prayers and, so surely riven
With the scent of the baking and glow, be driven
To expedients of praise to rustle through bins
Of platitudes for those that sing true as one spins
In a centrifuge of primrosing, to be pressed in a heaven
Of glowing compliments. Crust at the end
Is a premium for taste, warming the palm
As it makes one congenial. I must breathe a psalm
Or sing it sotto voce and say, maybe contend,
That nonesuch, no never, was it made ever better,
As now it arrives to the lips with melting butter.

Football Game

The announcer's voice weighs forward, grave
With import and evidence. But what transpires?
Knuckles loosen, jerking; a groin cracks;
A tendon rips away; redundant racks
Of teeth lean; noses smear; leading wires
Of mind jostle, thrumming in a case; pyres
Of pain spurt and char; a leg lacks
Resilience, breaks; eyes behold tacks
Of consciousness in day's vivid gyres
Of the Valkyrie; a skeleton rummages, stiff
Through itself, hunching; hernia and cartilage
Pop against a drum of air; and a midriff
Fails as the announcer indulges in persiflage
And notes coincidence. Guard and tackle sack,
Hang, and draw the quarterback. Offsides.
Call it all back and do it again.

Friday Night Movies

The recreation hall at the end of the street
Was a sepulchre for wishing until Friday night,
And then it came alive in the soft chrysolite
Of evening when the movies revealed the elite
Of Hollywood before us in scenes replete
With heroic empathy. Our wondering starlight
And aureole of soul seem wanton now, in spite
Of softening memory. But days one might delete
For their aridity movies once restored. Sallow
Days that slipped into crevices of recusing
Had the scintillance of Laurel and mellow
Hardy's wondrous antics that kept us musing
About absurdity and graced us for the machinery
Of even protocol and the dulling scenery
Of the world that rose before us.

Lady Bug

Plausible eft thing, a hemisphere of bug,
You afflict unedibles along a certain leaf
Where your duty is a universal cleanliness,
And if I should subject you to the press
Of dailihood, you would scrounge in disbelief,
Miffed at such a regimen. There on the jungle rug

You haul yourself in some pursuit of aphid,
I suppose. What must you run across but tack,
Causing you to swerve, even stumble, wobbling
On such tiny spindles sans shoes or even cobbling,
Minutely, slippers for your gliding. What you lack
In poise you gain in certitude, spotted lid

And spiritus convivial! Could I make a pet
Of you and keep you vigilant in other ways,
Such as a waker of the neighborhood, a chanticleer?
Such a soul needs expansiveness, not mere
Duty on a leaf or rug. Shall I arrange a maze
For you to master in which to let you whet

Your conscience for our rectitude? What fine pursuit
For businessing, for management control,
Comptrolling everything with petite and gentle
Humor, a resident chairless chairman on a lintel
To survey accounts! I think a plebiscite or poll
Among all denizens would get us better fruit

In a better Eden of your purpose and design.

Kitty Lucy Belle (1967–1985)

Lucy Belle, with your fur so white,
Where will you go to sleep tonight?
Stay calm and near whatever you do.
Your mistress keeps a place for you.

Malfare in Late October

Well, consider it, though you may not get it.
Spooks of halloween receive it well on dole,
Itching and fidgeting with varieties of soul.
Their indigence, their witchery must let it
Come, and imps with argument for sundering
Must invest it randomly in nooks of rookeries
Of pterodactyls where they prepare their claqueries,
To be. Vine the dark and musty hours, wondering
How they are, slipping and tracking, ratcheting
In blue and orange, with scary pumpkins glowing
Wickedly with teeth, with web of all our fears
Tattering through them. Formic denizens, sowing
Wind, reap our souls, like dervishes in weirs
Of air, and upstarts, acknowledging a weird
Electorate, fulfill some destiny to beard
Medusa as she pretties up for us with treats.

Cubig Dowd with a Cold

A malaise, a rustle of heat, and your sultry skin
Suspires as if conscious of itself. A tickle
In the throat persists into a twinge, and a sickle
Of pain meddles over surfaces of corrugated tin
As if it were dry from the heat of it. What tacit sin
Have you committed, so freighted in and fickle
To a disposition of hypocritic flames that trickle
Up your nose, impertinent and illogical. So pin
Or nail it where it is and scald it with camphor,
Breathing in. But it holds, already firm and old,
Intrenching a chink of disease. Fuming white of phosphor
Could burn it out and relieve you, but would fold
Nearby tissue into lesion. No. Get it and have it.
It is now of you, once at ease. You salve it,

Udavailig. You hack your story to a fetid durse,
Yourself, dot dowig how to clibe out or, flittig
Up, escape idto prestigious air add glow. Pittig
Aseptic spray agaidst a host of bolecules, you curse
A fortude that flees to field add hillock as you rehearse
Balaria. At the berest suggestiod of botif, whittig
Idto ad idcipiedt warble, kachoo!, viruses, as if dittig
Up your dose add stitchig it with little hooks, ibberse
The spodgy tissue of your head. Thed herpes sibplex,
Id ad evil residedce, bulges skid idto a softedig pad
That is allied to itself, but udified, add tickles dowd
Your lip idto codcocted reefs of paid that receive sad
Flow add ebb. Add eved though you thresh add drowd,

You do dot flex add die idto sleep, but darl your face
Udtil you blear add bubble, hydrophobiac, drippig lace

Of foab just adywhere.

Sweet Williab's Olde Cold

Dear Dorothy, hostest thou Sweet Williab, O,
Amid the raide, amid the wedde? Sayeth yes or no
    As I aske thee. Doth Sweet Williab lie abed,
Sodded so, lookige sparkly, eved so?

He is sowde* so easily. Set hib therefore oude aussi
In hotte July as bieddial, white and eved rosy,
    Eved pink as he now appeareth in Baye or June;
Sifte hib welle with sadd and soile. Lo, see

How nexte year he wille sproude if with draidage
In a potte thou givest hib full sud and full wage
    Of thy appreciacioud for his flourishige.
True leaves wille cobe, thed oude amid the sage

Move thou hib to ouddoor bedde with bultidibble
(Upside dowde like a bedde of dailes) and dribble
    Raide on hib for his happidesse, that once was loste.
If, though tempeste tost, bulch him with deedles and dibble

Pide codes for nuttes to while the dime. Froste
Wille cobe to no availe if, so carige, thou wast
    Circubspecte. Lo, how happy alle, dext sprig,
Whed uppe he cobes agaide. Forget the coste;

---

*Maddy tribs.

It wille be worthe it alle, what with such proliferacioud
For a poet's poebes! Thy neighbours, in such disstraccioud,
    Wille wedde uppe Suddigdale to see bright budches
Clusterige add fulfillige as the brighdesd collecticcioud

For their bright ibagidacioud, I fully wist!
(If nodde, checke with thy local botadiste.)

The Artful Dodgson, Storyteller for Children

Lewis Carroll, in lieu, is carolling,
Who must care for all in his role of being
Indirect and so able to effect his seeing
Well and saying well, writing, tolling
Wonder through the land as he is, trolling
Like a Giacomo at the court, unfleeing
From the Queen of Hearts and selling
Humpty Dumpty on his story, who told it
Little, only to get time for sitting
And listening, unified. Instead is, knitting
Pearling stories verbatim in lieu of. Hold it.
Now you have it right, as Lou is sunning
At Versailles. What's he good at? Punning,
Well! Wait and see like Alice ungrowing up
To meet the sun and sunning too.

Encounter

The brusque beginning of romance is a coincidence.
What then transpires is a delicacy that vain
Etiquette must muster: a hovering, hardly sane
As birdflight on a tether, or the incidence
Of perfume, or a prism's bright evidence
Of light, or faintest aspirations that wane
Into remembrance. What are they as they reign
Forward into forever? They keep weightily dense
Circumstance away, lightly carry a feather
Over a flower, over dew that settles there. Whether
It stays may be commitment, like an orient star
That fixes far reckoning. See the spar
That wavers over the sea? Far more stable,
The hint may be for ever, whether it seems stable,
Or not.

New Love

You come into this haven
Where glowing candles quiver
With your breath. You shiver
With my newest query, never
To know the certainty of heaven
For all the holy seven,
Eleven, or the clever
Strategies that love devises,
And none that it despises.
You freely move. You sever
Memories for this invention
That now demands attention.
I take you as you are,
As if to trace a star
That falls but does not perish,
Still aglow, but hesitant,
Though sure enough to cherish.

Adam

Green may merge into gold, but sans
A photosynthesis. Gold may be thin,
Thin as light hung in shimmering sin.
O apple, you loft, since light fans
From the sun, into a hand that tans
Into lustre and becomes a color akin
To gold the gilt of Apollo, whose kin
Are the lustre of Mycenae. Cannes
Of côté d'azur is a veriest name
For Eden down the panoply of fame
The sun may shine on. It is the same,
Now as then, the luxury of a breeze,
The breath against palms, the lees
Of love and languor, all in a frieze
Of being without her.

An Ingenuity

The sign is far along the way
And cannot easily be read
Until one approaches the cay
Of palms and the sunning overhead.

Away, the bridge against the mist
Vanishes into the denser white
That seems gardenia's whist
Sun, or as the softest night

That vanishes whisking away and down.
That gentleness becomes a will
Intransigent as the eastern khan
Who ministers along an early rill

In our meadowing. The earling youth
Accepts its pale translucency
And calls it part of living. The uncouth
Hours expunge it, but in his excellency

Of knowing not too much he suspends
The tapestry of galaxies where stars
Recess into the light, where light impends
As glory, and where our knowing chars

Unknowing and redundancy.

La Douce, or Flirt

A sleight may offer itself, smoothing
A vision of a shore. The shore, near the sea,
Becomes the sand. A rift of water slips across it.
So I take my fabric. Like my love, I emboss it
With my meditation. You came to me to see
A pattern in me like my dream, reproving
A flow that suggests it. Shall I touch my lace
Against your wrist, like fishnet floating near?
Come here. I draw you subtly as if you know.
And then you do. This is a harbor; so
Sand must glisten, almost mirror, sheer
As light of stars. These stars and just a trace
Of wind dim through. This far-flung shore
Keeps me. Hear me in the mist. This fabric
Use. It is smooth as fragile memory
Of light, soft as stars abroad in it,
And should you come, remember to win it
With a strategy. Accept the hint of magic
That I offer. Receive it, receive it as before.

Lover

Deep red and blue blend as shadows as each
Wanders through the other to gleam and reach
A sepulchre. You come to meet me, listing
To touch my hair. This magenta silence, misting
At evening, is full of suggestion, as if to teach
Desire as unity. Now, my love, your speech
Confuses me, though its savor, persisting,
Is sultry still. You come, almost insisting,
And I love you more and more as you breathe
A glow in me to flame, leaning into me.

A Relationship

At the gate at last, she hesitates to touch
The latch. A gloss of ribbon falls across
Her hand, and she lifts the latch, too much
Taken by what she sees. Can she toss

The ribbon either way like an ecstasy?
The giving as she comes is like a grace
That heaven offers, involving fantasy.
She knows me well, as I know the lace

Across her shoulders, not inwardly,
But there. What I have in mind
I cannot tell her, but frowardly
I exclaim that I am always kind,

Though my words are often bleak,
Or less than that, dull gray. I say
Them easily but parry, as I seek
Her love, to see how she will play

With them to feel what they will do
Between us. She endures me more than well,
Beyond compassion. What must be due
Is an investment I cannot sell

But one she knows, for I am less
An escort than I think and more
What she expects. She does not press
Commitment. She knows the subtle lore

I traffic in, and what's in store,
For she has heard it all before,
And sees it coming.

The Complication of Love

I am now in stereo, a couple's couplet,
A doublet mirror, taste in duplicate,
Surviving two, touch of us to replicate
Desire, rodomontade if one should let
Oneself bespeak another, to whom a debt
Is not as venerable as Mendelssohn's circlet
At an altar. So one alters nonesuch much
And rests awhile to survey that once hutch
Of oneself exponentially lonely, set
In that way as servilely nor, but now stet
In place near a fire, waffling our susurrus
Metabolically, such talking and tocking to hush
That we cannot disbelieve that we are so much like us.

Golden Frame: A Keepsake

From what period, one can guess, but the image
Is telling: possible 1810, 1842, or 1875, late,
Or even early. And so, exhibiting a trait
Of antiquity, it charms with the pretty visage
That graces it. Years can bend so in the cage
Of time if they serve veracity to curve in the elate
Scape and shore of light. Persimmon in the age
Of daffodils when spring was known gentles the sage
Of her pastel, for it is not age in her but the fate
Of such kept things in a chest, the silk of a dress,
A shoelace, a bow, and the tress that may hover
From a finger as it did over her eye to impress
Someone who loved her. That is why the cover
Of glass will protect her glory and her ecstasy,
And that is why love keeps her in a golden immediacy.

Vulnerable

An asking in the eyes, an ingenuous aura
In her hair, a suffusion about her as if a pane
Of milkglass had intervened to give her reign
In a meadow more credence: this is Laura.
One has seen such exuberance of curves in Cara
Stone move in the possession of spirit in the domain
Of current Rome and St. Peter's smoothing Seine
Of light that moves into celeste and the cathedra
Of the hills. She is winsome and reserves a plaint
That someone is neglectful, obviously wondering
How she will be attended as she, politely sundering
A reserve that I had planned but now seems a feint,
That I dismiss. For a very miss is she and lissomely
So vulnerable that I am taken aback, so handsomely
Rewarded by her being Laura only, all.

Meeting

She tosses an air into day,
Humming too. Whose bequest is she
But her own, not knowing? The French state it
For liaison, but my rousing lay
For her is silent, in my glance.

Commitment

Singe the air with evening's shade across the lawn.
Sun falls through and lengthens, kept aglow
By dwelling over green, the glow kept to show
The evidence of gold on green again. Dawn
May come to extend it against that flow, wan
Then shining and thinning as a ray. Low
On that horizon, cast higher still to sow
The morning, light to light, leaf tips drawn
To sun, the silver flickers into the verity
Of jewels of day. Ochre rises in between to play
Through green and brown as I commit myself to say
Hello. You smooth the green with the clarity
Of gold, west or east, palely with your touch;
Your lips, however sun may be much too much,
Come what may.

A Lasting Relationship

Just imagine! She took my arm
And nestled it longer than I thought
Appropriate in a ploy that was not
Platonic. Even the rustic farm
Nearby was befitting and hardly harm
For a full possession that she sought
For just a moment. Her subtle plot
Was a hesitation, implying a willingness
For yet another such encounter.
It happened once, and now I confess
That she has changed me. So I counter
All else with a prior downy vision,
Finding in me the quick decision
That I must marry her.

Casualty

Your perfume is a murmur one listens to,
Bracing me as if I were in a minuet
Turning, gesturing, but into a subtle darkness
Where a blaze flickers across the old faience
Of memory. If in this I am froward too,
I might bend a willow at a windy cape—
Where the surge is, wherein a welling starkness
Is, incorporate. I am so incorporate,
Dissembling what I was, shaken in a radiance,
An emanation deferring to the pretense
Of minor continuity. Now taken aback, I sift
A protocol to serve you. Your evidence
Confuses me, shimmering, welling like the sea!
I touch the air, and you, awaiting me,
A courier of languor like a sail adrift,
Waiting, waiting. And now for the taking, you lift
My bronze for a casual sating, now.

Sub Rosa Douce, or Flirt

A temptation may suggest itself, smoothing
Like an image of a shore. The shore, near a sea,
Becomes sand. A rift of water slips across it.
I take my fabric. Like my love, I emboss it
With my meditation. You came to me to see
A pattern in me like my dream, reproving

The glance that suggested it. Shall I touch my lace
Against your wrist, like fishnet floating near?
Come here. I draw you subtly as if you know.
And then you do. This is harbor. So
Sand must glisten, almost mirror, sheer
As light of stars. These stars and just a trace

Of winds dim through. This far-flung shore
Keeps me. Hear me in the mist. This fabric
Use. It is as smooth as the very memory
Of light, soft as stars abroad in it,
And you should come, remembering to win it
With a strategy. Accept the hint of magic
That I offer. Receive it now, as my lore.

A Romance

As if a touch through distance,
Communing is a ghostly levitation
That comprises the holy station
For our wishing it could be. A trance
Would not do as well, or even the dance
Pavane. In the rose of its creation,
It is quick as dew limpid in elation,
Glancing to the eye for the chance
To continue further, as a droplet
Does on a petal, immerging into air
That softens mistily in a wavelet
Of the sun. I see you watching, fair
Amid the concourse, me. Our we
Is the we we know that assembles three,
The Ghost of love one of them, then "we."

Love's Resonance

Hear it now: thou me, in us, together.
When was it otherwise ingenious? The rising
Sound in me is thee empirically the empire
Of a contradiction now a one, for a fire
Is burning as a pyre of fusion devising
This centrality. See the blue of whether

We can make a trial of faith a resonance
Up a register where a simple ligature
Makes the name of one so indivisible.
And is there an accordion for the risible
To play upon, with several keys falsetto
To give us pause in this consonance?

A Dream

Romance is a gauze. The gauze is translucent,
Aswarm with glitter, and the glitter is starry,
Or dusty with distance, or dust itself. I carry
It in dreams, dreams of my dreaming, nascent
In hours of lakemist along the shore, in the scent
Of flowers in water. Along the path a faery
Emerges, or psyche adrift in air, sorry
With sadness, alone. She drifts to repent
Of her Asia, bereft of the lingering sagerose
In my hand. If she would take it in the haze,
The mallows of light would descend in the praise
Of morning. In the light that may come, she knows
The vane of the hours, when the past flows
Away, when she is here, transpiring from dreams.
She is the gloss and movement of satin, what she seems,
And all else now reality, a dream, as I awaken
To know it as the haze now gone, now gone and forsaken.

Wedding Morn

One bloom tips against another near the sea,
And light passes over it as if in a vision.
Shadows pass to and fro in the elision
Of the sky, where vision is, fair to see,
In fantasy. He had pulled at her glove,
And off it came. And then her fingers
Played in a truancy from love. He lingers,
Watches, touches, takes them, like love
In its circumambience of knowing. Touch
Is becoming, fleet with its burden, such
Faerie lore as with bluebells and larkspur,
Touching. She looks up coquettishly,
But knowing, having seen, in the lea
Of a glory, him, in a glimpse, to lure
Him to her. Just a touch, enough to inure
The practice of yielding where seawinds flee
Along the coast, across headland and bay, free
To send crests surpassing blue, to endure
The sea-island rock and to wash into ravine
And storm. Afterwards, they keep a sheen
Of mirrors of mist that pass away before they walk
To an edge for a venue of regrettable candor.

An Old Record

"Lights . . . lights are low since you went away."
The refrain, the refrain played on a gramophone.
It was old as a disparate glissando in tone
Of silence restored in the memory to stray
Against memory to nurture the soul to play
Over the strings of a viol. Over its form shone
The melody as if a melody could own
A transparency and, so, an eternal lay
That suggested a love. How can a metaphysics stay
The value of a resonance that is its own authority?
How can a sentiment arouse the depthless surety
Of myth? Love was then, and then the very ray
Of translucent being: myth one knows, but knows
Only from its being, untranslatable except as prose
Becomes the song of poetry since you went away.

Memory of a Garden

How was it forgotten? Old estates beside
Each other were nearly so, and, when taken
Into the fold of an aristocracy, were not forsaken
But lived in tenuously, as if, in a way, to deride
The past. The tenants looked around as if denied
Access even to the way to Woburn Abbey, shaken
In their temerity for living near. Some awaken,
Others do not, and living was a flicker in a stream
That occurs again. A gate nearby remained between,
Unopened, even undisturbed, and beyond in the sheen
Of early memory of a century ago. And so I dream
Of it as it was in England, and I am nearly sure
It remains so, even though its society might demur

To think beyond its time. The gown I see is small,
Of that other time, in the gravure of afternoon.
It moves in another dance, as specks of dust assume
A lightness. Who is there, in the whisper of tall
Elms acluster near the wall? Their shadows fall
Eastward into night. How can time, in their room
Of my remembrance, so complain as fairly to loom
Into the present? Illusion rests near the wall
Of memory. Memory lies short of any knowing.
It lies there kept, as we were, passing, glowing.

Guy Coleman: The Singer of Midway

One cannot take Provo Canyon and Heber Valley idly except to vacation in them. From the forty-five hundred feet of Utah Valley to the almost six thousand of Heber Valley is a lyrical passage rising like a birdsong: the turns of the canyon, the treble cleft of rock shaped eons ago, the mountain valleys above the edge of waterfalls, the pinnacles of rock and snow, the cliffs on either side rising to abutments and sloping in, the shafts of green, the moraine, the river widening to grassy banks and knolls, the acres of brown-golden grass in summer, and then the dam at the height of water that stretches far against slopes and islands reaching to the Valley and to Charleston.

I'm not sure, but I think Charleston was named by a settler who thought of England and its royal dignity. One goes to the left through this hamlet of sheep and cows, white houses and chalets, into the village of Guy Coleman—Midway, Utah. As one approaches the main intersection, he sees immediately FOE, though the startling negative reading of the letters certainly makes them seem inappropriate there. The lodge of the Elks therein is a chalet with a constant attendance of bright pickup trucks and automobiles. On the northeast corner lives Lethe Tatge in her red house with its Victorian white scrolls abounding along the eaves. She looks crotchety, but actually isn't. She is rather more like the matron of the proverbial shoe, but with little more to do than entertain travellers who inquire at her door. Two enormous pine trees make the house seem enforested. On the southwest corner is a brick bungalow that must have been built in the twenties. There on the northwest corner is a petite self-serve gas station and, beside it, a cubicle that serves as a store. The proprietor is known for his curly hair, mild manner, and inveterate smile. He will sell customers washer fluid, oil, instant-hot sandwiches, penny candy, and popcorn that brims and bustles yellow under glowing lights. Next door, west, is the famed store of the erstwhile Welshman, Guy Coleman. It has a white face, and above the long window and swinging doors is his name in great italics: *COLEMAN'S*.

Through the swinging doors and in, one sees Guy, the poet, selling groceries to such people as the Kohlers, the Lences (formerly "Lenz"), the Probsts, the Neerings, the Tuckers, the Springers, the Hubers, the Sweetens, the O'Driscolls, the O'Tooles, the Provosts, the Mahoneys, and others, I think, of the Celtic revival. If they should get along together any better than they do, one might imagine them to be congenial elves from the forests of Europe who had banded together in this new land to support the elfin fantasies of Barrie and Shakespeare. Midway is a transmutation, if not a transliteration. It is fabled almost without knowing it. The nineteenth-century pioneers of the valley, some at one end, others at the other, got together, as a protection against now-vanished Indians, and called the place "Midway," in the spirit of congenial location and conciliation. The spirit has endured owing to natural good will, but chiefly owing to the fact that Guy Coleman, the erstwhile Welshman and Midway's poet, knew how to make the most of it. He lived in Midway for the peace it brought him, and he achieved it beautifully, magnificently, though he was ofttimes lonely as an owl in a loft, especially at the end of the swing shift in his store. And he kept the peace better than any justice of the peace could. Even the city council learned that they were surrogates of his good will and diplomacy. Such a diversity of cultural background might intimate the possibility of a feudalism, but not with Guy around, supervening with his poetry and camaraderie.

I see him as if yesterday were today. I notice his book of poems at the corner of his counter, at the nearest point to his customers as they open their wallets and purses after having reached over the poems with their groceries to place them on his counter. His volume of poems, *Pine Whispers and Autumn Leaves,* lies open. I casually read:

> I have no complaint—sincerely I pray
> That if another place is being prepared for us
> That it contains lush mountain valleys and singing
>   mountain streams,
> A Timpanogos,
> Beautiful canyons, green groves of pine and aspen,
> Ferns and wild flowers and humble grass,
> A carpet of maple and oak,
> And cottonwoods along a quiet river,
> A change of seasons . . .
> A land peopled with those I love . . .

> *   *   *

> Came a clarion call from the valley,
> From the wind and the lithe willow tree
> To the tremulous forests of aspen . . .

Guy has turned from the artifacts and condiments that so please children and contentedly, silently, watches me read. I sense that he knows me for my English-Scotch, Norwegian (non-Welsh) ancestry, and for my bookishness. I notice askance that he smiles. The place is quiet, the sunlight through the window giving the potato chips, the bananas, the lettuce, and the milk a spring-like glow. His hair is silvery white, reminding me of a godly oracle. His face is so rounded and his skin is so clear that he seems beatified, like an elf who has been recently dubbed a Christian of Glamorganshire. His eyes, implacably even and perceiving, seem to contain whatever he sees, and his lips, precise and calm, seem to wait for what I might offer as a comment about my reading. Altogether, he reminds me of a freshly baked loaf of white bread.

He asks whether I like his poems, and I say, indeed, yes! We discuss them for a while, I nodding and nodding, dreaming and listening, as his English spins out like silk, diphthongizing and flowing, and for a moment I imagine myself listening to Merlin. The potato chips look even brighter than before.

He says, "Don't get old. I don't want to leave Midway. What would I do without it? Oh, Pete, my son, will assume the ambiance here. So I don't worry about that."

"Where are you going?" I ask lamely.

He looks evenly at me, at first not answering.

He says, "My wife is sick, and I can't do without her."

The pines at Tatge's corner seethe from the wind that arose from the lake three miles away.

He says, "Since the dam was built in the thirties, Midway has been cooler."

My reverie is ended.

El Dorado, or Shangri La, even here, could not be eternal. Timpanogos, distant across the crystal-blue water, misted with sun and clouds. The deep greens of the hillsides resembled pine frost in a sunlit glade. I gazed at it, not really noticing him as he turned to his cash register and installed my money for a copy of his book.

I mused about him as I left and travelled up Center Street.

His son, I remembered, was most helpful, but unsuccessful, in helping me to acquire from the commissioners of Wasatch County a perfect, unused copy of *Webster's Second International Dictionary* that I had seen on a high shelf in the Treasurer's office. I thought that both Guy and I could have used it, on occasion. Having it would have provided another reason for my chatting with him above and beyond the commercialism involved in buying groceries.

On my way to my acre up Center Street, images of Cardiff, Ebbw Vale, Cyfarthfa Castle, and Merthyr Tydfil seemed at hand, as if in some medieval time when the Welsh were farmers and herdsmen only, or in a time before that, when Joseph of Arimathea brought the Holy Grail to Wales for holy believing, endowing the Welsh with their natural talent for poetry.

Midway is known for its tufa, called "pot rock." It is a fairly soft rock that can be found abundantly on hills and fields. Many of Midway's prominences look like natural beehives, rounded, almost perfectly shaped knolls that often emit steam. In them, or exposed, is hot mineral water that offers convections of soul-inspiring warmth when applied to the skin. One may sit in "hot pots" and receive the ultimate rest of Nirvana. And one may heat his home with it if it is accessible.

The official "hot pots," Schneitter's, were a Mecca for health addicts and philosophers. Added to them were picnic areas, a golf course, niches for camping amid the aspens and pines, stables for recreational horse riding, a marina for boats and windsurfing, and the "Heber Creeper," a steam engine and railroad cars behind it that would take three trips daily, during the summer, beside the lake and down the canyon to Bridal Veil Falls.

Cascade Springs is higher, at eighty-five hundred feet, an extrusion of the water table, the lowest point of which is Utah Lake, in Utah Valley, at forty-five hundred feet. These are a few of the accoutrements of Midway, and the citizens, well aware of them, protect their heritage with a fine propriety, sometimes excessively, with a touch of resentment for any persons who might seem inclined to take undue advantage. One must construe some attitudes as evidence of xenophobia.

Guy often hinted to those exhibiting such evidence that they seemed perfectly at ease to travel to Buena Park and Anaheim, California, to visit the facilities of Disneyland without compunction and without the objection of residents of those cities. They would seem abashed and skulk home to think awhile. Once a fellow sauntered in and indicated that the economy of Midway was falling apart because new residents were buying appliances not here, but there, in the malls along the Wasatch Front, over the mountains. Guy asserted that often he himself would sell and transport refrigerators, stoves, etc., to customers in those same places, so please, would he shush and stop the caterwauling. Things were going very well, indeed. Midway would be the same, though hard top had replaced the dirt paths and roads.

He struggled to establish, as a consistent code, the Greek heritage of sweet reason, and he was hard pressed when some descendant of Prussia would march into Coleman's and assert that the sewer district was all wrong. Guy assured him that the substances flowing in the pipes would be duly purified in three stages until the emergent water at the far end of the district would be almost fit to drink and in no wise would pollute his herd of cows, or him. Placated, he would click his heels and disappear.

"Swiss Days" is a vast experiment in camaraderie conceived and produced by the citizens, and it was Guy's universally-accepted option to modulate the affair. What a bazaar for cuts of knockwurst and salami, for Swiss haberdashery, for sandals, for apple pie à la mode, and for wood carving, for portraiture and yodelers and cloggers! In the evenings the family Britsch would carry the audiences into stints of euphoria with musicals. Two voices, somehow matched to a fare-thee-well, Britsch would use in a musical skit emphasizing alpine echoing. The lyrics would rise as high as birdsong or the lilt of a waterfall.

Guy would stand in his cubicle in the store, twinkling with mood upon mood, giving directions to strangers. And especially at the chuck wagon breakfast, he would mill with the crowd. Swiss Days, owing partly to him, never lost its piquancy, its Swiss zest, its panache, its genuineness. His eyes would sparkle like firelight, and it seemed that the legends of faraway Wales came there with a vibrancy, and the wisps of steam from the hot pots would waft into the sky like the Eumenides, blessing the town.

A madness descended in Guy when the plaques on Memorial Hill were vandalized. Thinking of him, I read his poem "Gently France," which begins:

> O hold him gently, soil of France,
> And kindly vigil keep.
> Our soldier lad lies in thy fields,
> Lies in thy arms asleep. . . .

I knew that Guy was consoling himself in the same way, that the plaques were ways of remembering the soldiers, but that they really resided in the immortality of spiritual conviction to be established forever in the regency of the paradisal world of the Millennium.

One day I went to his store for milk. I looked back up Center Street and imagined Guy and wife, Teresa, walking steadily toward Interlaken, a spread of storied chalets nestling in a col, as it were, of a mountain. It was evening, and the lights sparkled a homeyness of communion. Guy and Teresa vanished in a curve of the road.

In the store, I found Guy disconsolate.

"She's gone," he said, as simply as that. "I can't stay behind. The viewing is tomorrow, before the graveside services."

"Guy," I said. "Your poetry is filled with the spirit that she still lives beside you."

"Yes," he said. "But the ache remains in me, and I want to go."

"But your Midway is as fine as ever. Timpanogos looks like frosted crystal under a new moon."

"Listen," he said, opening his book. He went on, reading aloud:

> I want to be there
> In the opaque of death's night
> In the silence and the gloom.
> I want to be there
> To welcome my loved ones
> Who may be confused
> Who may be afraid
> Crossing the dark river.

Somehow, by way of contrast, I thought of the legends of Greece, of the fate of Greek heroes, of Achilles and Agamemnon.

"No," I said to him. "Think of the light wind in the aspens."

I left. He turned to his register, almost dozing as he clicked it shut.

I was gone from Midway for weeks. When I returned from Anaheim to the solace of Midway, Pete was in the cubicle.

I said, "Where's your father, Pete?"

And he said, "He's gone. We buried him beside Mother last Tuesday."

I suppose that Guy is gone. But if he is there, in the opaque night, he is brightening it up like the stars over Interlaken, with his poems in his hands, reading and offering them to his family, to the veterans of wars, to Captain Springer, John Sulser, John Morton, Peter Abplanalp, Joe Galli, Eph Mohmlan, Tattersall, Levigneur, Alfred Alder, and to many other denizens that lived in this newest Wales.

Well, Guy, back to my reverie. I wanted to talk with you further, but I do not see you around as much as I used to, except in the colors and sounds of your valley. Not too long ago, last August the tenth, I think, the leaves of the valley were heavily dusted, what with so many campers accosting the forest rangers for parking spaces. That night the northwest rains came and washed the leaves sparkling clean. I knew you would not mind my recording what I saw in an *essai* about it, in an attempt to honor you for what you love. I would not want to keep you from your work and your glory, but stop rustling for a while and listen:

AUTUMN LEAVES

Dust of the summer weeks appalled the evenings,
Settling like peace into the russet plain
As a leveller of hues:

                      now earthtone leavenings
Float into the hill, and the empress cloud
Rails, trailing rain—rain, dint of high storm
Reviving light, then the lancet diagonal spurts
Of rain to dust. It takes from the spectrum
Rainbow gusts of light, and the rise and span
Of trees vanish in turbulence, the rainwind
Veering lower in the silver dusk.

                                 Hours
Of rain wash the concourse of the autumn leaves
In hours of night, and as dawn fields visions
Of the arriving day the leaves, in that intensity,
Leave grey and assume the shine of water
Freshening fine in the diamonds of spray,
Then in the thrust of light their fire!

Matte and patina dull, as once they were,
Because from russet topaz, from rust carmine,
From saffron aureate gold, from dun emerald,
From azure amethyst blue, smooth as the lake
In the silence of light, smooth as the fielding
Sun, aureate of hours modulating hues in flashings
Of ridges to rockwall promontories and heights
Of the sky: gems in the suddenness of dew,
Misting swatches of yellow-gold, gold in the lighter
Green, green in brown, brown at the edge, the cardinal
Vale there like a wind, violet in deeper mauve,
Mauve in grey stone, earthbrown sills higher and higher.

Spun in the gestures of color, ambient as the breeze
Reveals outcropping stone:

                                aspens awakening in the surge
Of the sun's early wind, turning and fluttering leaves
Across vertical white strands in the plenum
Of their stand against the mountain, the mail
Rain still there, but coasting over margents of blue
Into the freer blue of sky, the sound of paling light. . . .
Autumn! and this from the steel twilight of rain!

All this will fall into the matte earth's engendering
Loam, rich black annealing soil.

                               Sails of color wander
Under clouds beyond this immediacy of wind,
Shadowy dim in the heights of space, and where is
The ultimate variety from the reign that will rinse
The sheen of the spiritual stars, the blue-white gems
Of polar winds wherein all glory flickers
As the autumn of stars, leafing as highlights,
Wends across the spectral forest of light?

Guy, after reading my own poetry about your valley (and please
pardon any intrusions of mine upon your prerogatives) and
after mulling further over your book, I see more clearly what
you were about in your cubicle. Your fellow townsmen were
descendants of pioneers who, because they shared a great vision
and a great belief, left Zurich, Basil, Geneva, Alsace-Lorraine,
Dresden, Munich, Copenhagen, Warsaw, Danzig, Stockholm,
Oslo, Paris, Amsterdam, Wilhelmshaven, Trondheim Fjord,
London, Cherbourg, Cardiff, Cobh, Marseilles, Dublin, and
Swansea to come to America, to come far west after they
arrived, through Boston, Williamsburg, New York, St. Louis,
Omaha, and Saint Joe, to find themselves, at last, struggling
with oxen and wagons on the plains of Nebraska. You know

how it went there. The Oregon Trail offered its problems. Constantly, incessantly, these pioneers walked, rose, pulled, and pushed down one hill, then up another, except that the next hill was always, almost always, higher than ever before. They came to North Platte, and when they saw the Great Divide in front of them, that ranges up to eight or nine thousand feet, their hearts sank within them. They had to take their precious things, things of great cultural value, and lay them gently beside the Trail: organs, Dresden ware, portraits of families to whom they had said goodbye forever, volumes of poetry like those of Milton, Herrick, Shakespeare, Chaucer, Spenser, and many, many memories too, and even loved ones in graves, who had died along the way. And then the great ascent into the clouds far in the distances, to the north the great peaks of the Tetons, and to the south the rolling hills and the canyons down to the Great Basin of the West. These ancestors found their way to a place that reminded them of Switzerland, Heber Valley, and they stayed, bereft of almost every acquisition of this world. You kept them together, Guy, and they stay together. Those who leave because they must, remember your valley and often return. You were like the ancient Welsh who gave Europe the blessings of Christianity and the wonders of the imagination when the great art and literature of Alexandria, Jerusalem, Athens, and Rome faded into forests of the Middle Ages. But the poetry remained as a transmutation of glory in the sagas of Charlemagne, the Cid, Deirdre and Naisi, King Arthur, Siegfried, Parsifal, and Geoffrey of Monmouth, all of whom remind one, as one considers them, of the Origin in Bethlehem. You gentled your townsmen in that glory, Guy, though many books and artifacts were lost on the plains.

Bless you, and let me take a page from your book and read it again.

Guy Coleman, After Teresa's Passing

Teresa, saint, you free the clouds into salient blue.
I guess your place where the avenues ascend
Into a curve. North star near, you send
A radiance for my reckoning. I drew
You once from Arcturus where darkness does not ensue
At night in the stellar brightness you lend.
Lend me, now, composure. I cannot stay to find
Dark shadows that move in rooms to strew
My patchwork memories. We walked away
So dreaming that we forgot the play of aging
In pallor, in the luxuriance of what to say
Next as smaller talk, having whispered, engaging
Youth again, we thought, yet shaking
With surprise that we could sense time breaking

Thin, and wisping. Teresa, I whistle morning
Into being as I did then. But now it loses
Lilt of song and settles in a mind that chooses
Silences and reminisces in starlight. A warning
Hushes me close into myself in my adorning
Sentiment. My loneliness is as strange, bruises
My emptiness where it fails, where it refuses
Solace. It reaches for you where a scorning
Jay wings down. The consort of these fields shirrs
His wings, abrades with chattering. Down by the river,
A path will dim away. I see you there. The giver
And redeemer whispers, almost here, and lures
Me to your side.

Affluent Entertainers

Smooth as honey or elixir,
What they issue will not bestir
Objection. Their plots are thirty-two,
And each will please, whatever you do
Or are. Receive them in decibels
Of 10, that they will bring you risibles
Aplenty, and you, in seeking parity,
Will choose them as a rarity
Of talent when they tell you so,
Who have shills to bell you so
For having money, rippling. Dandle it
Before you near them. Let them candle it
To see its quality. Smooth it
Down and watch them soothe it
Under Usura.

At a Writers' Conference

She perched on her chair, leaning slightly forward
To examine a common ground like a sparrow or wren,
But adequate to hear the rustling of certain prey.
Certainly, therefore, alert to disquisition or ploy,
Or innuendo, or meliorism, or what might have been
Before it was guessed—ready even for the froward

Light of intellect. But could she, in seeing, detect
Academia, the sloping intrigue of conversation
That isolates naïveté even before it wisps
Into view? Thin, sinewy, emaciate, her wrists
Might carry her weight if she fell in her inclination
To revise. Her poem, freighted in hand to deflect

Attention away from his venue, but professionally
There in a sheaf, was next for review. The verdict
Preceded the critic as an air he pushed in ahead
Of his gusto for calumny. He was gray as sage
On the desert floor, for he would slowly interdict
Her felony, that she should write at all so menially

Or without slight education. He rousted her guilt
With grammar and logic, but one remembers pleonasm
In Housman and accent in Chaucer. She was violate,
Enough for pillory, and got it, head and hands to sate
The attention of laughter, that was sane. See the spasm
Of lids, the purple temple, the start, but the gilt

Scroll of his critique! He pranced in the room
As her metaphysic gleamed starlight, the dream
Of her witness. One has heard of critic Lessing,

The connoisseur, but this, above all, was chessing
To advantage, well upstage. Before him, to seem
Urbane of him, was another, mistress in tights, in the tomb

Of indelicacy for all, to be ignored, as he flouted
The poem with his indignation, that she could conceive
Of such tripe before these beloved of writers, here
On this campus of our blessed humanism, in the weir
Of such importance, of relevance, she having taken leave
Of her wit to submit poor minus D. He pouted

And slammed it as if it were merd, or spread
Of infamy that would not do. But a certain guest,
There for an hour, listened to her myth and tone,
And saw that her imagery of sight and bearing could atone
For the world of regularity: gray-violet west
Into sunset, talisman of sun, the dusky red

Of sacrifice, the array of the Bible, belief,
And the presence of Caedmon, praying his genesis,
To be the ancient singer, the singer of court,
Or of Arthur, shields around the table, the consort
Of Guinevere and then of glory, or of the hysteresis
Of Donne. The critic did not sense them, his sheaf

Waving in hand, paroxysm reigning far, and there.
She sank in dismay, in the crouch of her soul's mind,
Down under his stamping, as renegade, chipping
Detritus as if it were steel, inwardly ripping
Presumption into tatters of guilt where she might find
Remorse of the criminal in his creation, in the fear
Of destruction, deep in the red of an evil lore.

Atwit

Presently, it is near the ground, with wheels.
Porsche. Red. A roadrunner fumbles, in a stall,
For looking querulously at it, then away, wall-
Eyed and chagrined. He leans forward, anneals
The air with implicit speed. Steadier, he steals
Another look. A Maserati, with the shawl
Of a madonna on its leather. All this to appall
My penury as I, defensive as my creels,
Burn out with eccentricity as a Jaguar crouches
Near a pool of the jungle where a tempter purrs
Her terms in terms of score. Fiat accompli slouches
At the curb. Mine. Mercedes, in the gorgeous furs
I array her with in my wishing, swishes near,
Sold. Which is mine? The Audi, altered
As a racer? Do I believe myself, deferred

For another time, another place, shekeled cool
In Vegas, glittering with the chrome I saunter near?
Shell out, I confirm, lolling as I languorously peer.
A Lotus near the parkway rounds the pool,
Gliding, aquiver in the lights of sands, a rule
Of glamor I inveigh against my condition, mere
Before the exchequer and the chips where I steer
Myself into my cornered assets, cowering, to mewl
For access to that sleek Lamborghini rustling
Near Ferrari, who came to sell it. I whine
In one, with keys, so still after hustling
From my rustling Fiat, all atwit and bluffing,
Missing excelsior, puffing as I mutter, muffling

May day as an aficionado lost in cost and perjury,
Releasing funds enough to live in penury,

With hardly a chirp from me, or a twit.

Bigot

Start up his mill of cast iridium,
The manganese, the lead, the cesium.
His advocacy of logic is a constant wheel
Flinting against a substitute for steel
That flows with little heat. Conceal
Him in his place. He speaks the word
That firms and thickens like a curd
Of certainty, that soon becomes the merd
That slows us. He has his eerie bird
Of ego nestled low against the tedium
That he has settled, as the medium
Of his exchange, upon us, while fletching
Himself with eider eidolon or retching
The psychiatry of his inveterate delusions
To sun them publicly with his conclusions.

The Editorial Staff of

Playbuoy, etc., in a bunny warren, illicits
Centerfolds, cannily trims taffy edges
To the limits of fragile heresy, and dredges
Up any excuse as the PTA committee posits
What it should not do, but does. Requisites
Urging its defection precede oaths of pledges
For moral coda about reclusive skin. Who hedges,
Nevertheless, to receive the green for perquisites
So casually earned? Publishing is meringue of reason
For the slickering intimation of revealing sex.
Editor, to wit, opines self-righteously like Rex
Of the Mardi Gras. What will they get in the season
Of recompense for inventing the art of his ease
And so expertly perfecting a psychosomatic disease
That wriggles up and in and around like a spirochete?

Fred Astaire and Ginger Rogers

With the proficiency of a bending willow, he takes
Her by the waist and dips her, overbending,
And glides like savoir faire for all our sakes
Into episodes of easy motion and extending
Grace with such obvious panache he breaks
The commonplace into sticks and bits, sending
Dreams as barter for better ones, strewing flakes
Of color to glitter like pastel leaves wending
Earthward to be among us. Whatever makes
Existence is so improved, whatever impending
Glamour nearer us. His glance forsakes
All else but her as he lifts her over lakes
Of halftone blue below heavenly-attending
Indigo. Pale starlight of the sun's pretending
Seems a dimming glow as he enfolds and takes
Her lightly away for keeping and suspending
In magenta, shimmering. His tie is white,
His tuxedo flowing black, his ease of night
The evidence and preeminence of their lending
To the shadowing of light the spindrift shadows
Of a solitaire.

Fred Astaire, d. 1987

His feet are still. The tick, tick, tat, tat,
Tap, tap, shh . . . on sand, sand on floor,
The ruse away as if on seedling spindrift
Settling here and there, and then sans rift
Of soul or sound in the dancer's lore,
And this an early aspiration, as if one were Cat

Ballou. I ought to take a course in it to know
How it was done. If one had the will, and will
The talent, talent touch, and touch the grace,
Would it come? Not likely, though saving face
Might make one try. But he exhibited still
The rising style that meant to lift the flow

Of being into the angel of an angel's fire
Transmuted into mortal form, a form unique
In the panoply and exegesis of his meaning.
Never once again, as if Galahad were leaning
In the origin of light and seeking what to seek
In this dispensation in the glory and the pyre

Of our illumination.

Morrey the Fox

Having been a member of a team
(Which was morely is than seem),
This fox was Morrey of the Sox
Of Boston rather than a fox
(Nat'l Parker in Yellowstone).
He, tired as tired to the bone,
Had come much fagged and vitiated
From thinking (much exacerbated),
That he could fly, predicated
And surely highly vindicated
As to sense, you know. Morrey
(More than saying so) was not sorry
He was showy. For in the Park
Were, abounding, to bear and lark
Him easily, some to disprove
Him across the greensward or to improve
Him in the grass. But he lurked,
And, though bear and lark perked
Up, he was ready. Off he streaked,
His innate interest riled and peaked,
To soar, and did. Higher arch
Never was conceived, from noon to dark
Masterfully so executed, again,
Again, ears erect, with sen-sen
On his breath and very ready,
And, though remarkable and steady
With rules for flying, legs retracted,
He failed. Gravity soon exacted

Recompense. But would he fly
Morely? Yes! though occasionally wry,
Not once, but severally, alas,
Still very wily in the grass.

Great Pundits Decide
the National Team Standings

What we have, back east, is a meringue of id,
Who you are, what you are, where you are,
Whom you know. Way out here, a team must jar
Down ratchets of their favor, out for bid,
Then sold into Egypt. Pundits, on which a lid
Is never fixed, are among the media, far, O far
Into the ultimate. A bettor backs them in the tar
Of his opinion, with nodding odds, getting rid
Of preying variance. An outrider team is prey
For him, no name, no chance, and so is minuscule
In distant standings, and offers little fuel,
Little interest. O loss, O loss, we have no sway
At all, put down and out, except for some debacle
In a world of punditry—disruption like a miracle
From lesser media. Hail, Mary. Our team, in a way,
Is winning, with a perfect record rankling pundits.
O sanctus, pundits, unto us, for you, like bandits
Now transmogrified, deal us smalling happy words.

In the Precincts of the University

I entered the precincts where a visitation
Might be reasonable, past the mistletoe,
Where an oak receded into the height of evening.
The Breezeway of Computer Science lay ahead.
One could hear the rustling and subtle breathing.
Hushed phrases stilled into dark recesses.
I inspected the doors and the tags of identity,
And the office hours. The nigre marks of trauma
Where evident, and the listing of conditions
That were used to service those who waited
For conferences general or severally intimate.
"Condition: critical," read one who was astute
And fearing dressing down. The hint of lysol
Wafted at the opening of a door, with debris of chewable
Mints. A freshman came strolling out, head
Hanging after a deprecation. His theme he kept
Unto him, under his arm. He fled into a portico,
Where coeds held sessions of the orders of merit,
Solemnly winking. The next door read, "Fair"
For an associate professor who had a weakness
That was bruited at assemblies of the intimate,
But otherwise seldom known. He had considered
Penitence, but the very idea ragged his days
Into a prurience of detail. Another read, "Probation,"
Where the harried exacerbated neural tension
Into flippancy. Shadows meandered in gowns,
With protocol. The next read, "Satisfactory."
And he was, long known for his mien and endurance,
Though he would never rise to glittering ranks.

He could raise himself on fours to utter devotions
And listen to vespers at a nearby window.
The next read, "Very Critical" and "Intensive
Care," where a horrid flame commanded rhetoric
That ranged like the Valkyrie over a domain
Of ragged books. Who would pay the grievous toll?
Memoranda trilled out to dean and dean at bay
And palely shaking. And Cerberus roamed, lounging,
With a cigarette lolling to indicate contempt
For members of the junior staff, drawn into nitre
By his breath. What venom might his care incise?
The next read, "Stable," and inside stacks
Of résumés were replicate by reams, and growing
Still. Pray hallows here for them all, living
Inebriate in power amid the latest versions and editions
Of *The Prince* they use to get away from there.

Assigning a Freshman Theme

We are official, now by degrees, at school,
Self-conscious by degrees in our own selves, volatile
Of assertion, but accurate and precise, nubile
Of intellect, or opinionate. Where is the rule
But here, and now? We are elate, and this is yule,
A nativity of opportunity, our minds prehensile
As officialdom, with particular style,
Here collegian. Write an essay from some spool
Of recollection. Remember home and mother?
Why did you come here, matriculate for study?
Why are you rooming, grooming with your buddy
Near the HUB? Why do you row or smother
Lingua franca at the outset, in Seattle?
Write a theme for me and start this solemn battle
I shall win.

The Jeweler's

The prim flowers in the shoppe appoint themselves
To an iteration. The glass reflects them with angles
And prisms that rest against superficies in tangles
Of bright pastels. A hand that touches them helves
Their brilliance broadly. I count them in twelves
Or sevens or threes deftly to be holy. Spangles
Cross novae under glass, and a bluestone dangles
From a pendant. One admires the array of shelves
Of carats, wishing one, but, looking very just,
One wanders aisles in a fine diplomacy, affecting
An affluent air. One flows with the color, inspecting
Glitter at any moment. Having immerged from the must
That filters down the city, one dallies in this haven
Of a glazier who dusts gems, or rhinestones, like leaven
Over gold.

Politicized

Who is this holy terror
So secular and humanist
Who flouted the candid mirror
And flaunted the unraised fist?

Staff

To the left, captain of the notes that follow.
More than major, drum or domo, he bustles
Frontally into our attention and hustles
Prestige for music. He is a fellow
Of a saintly cloth and will not wallow
Like a rest. Therefore he rustles
When ill at ease, flexing muscles
To exacerbate a lovely mallow
Of a lyric passage of some Mozart.
He is the maestro's domo, ahead
Of fitting tone. In his bright stead,
He announces the paradigm and the art
That, as a tremor, makes one start
Or calm.

Prime Time Personae
at This Point in Time

Siva, what do they have in common? A sacred cow
That they urgently entail to quash responsibility.
The jilts, so luminous in their dire nubility,
Try to score with verbiage to exhibit and endow
Their Presences with vaster clientele. To plow
It up and ply it is their endearment and civility;
They learned to deck you with it as a risibility
That gained a status, then two or three, as a way
To vacate mind. The gurus ply it too, certainly
Enough for one to excoriate them. Hair must lay
Against a temple to typify a scene so wantonly
An affront, though they may not sense it. A cay
Leeward of them will serve. To sit there for a day
To receive the belling wind! But who can dismay
These anchors who try to hook you on the news,
Or hang it in on you, as claque for all you know?
Siva, only you.

Television Anchor Man

I am a stick on which to assemble clothes;
My flesh is air under pressure from the fan
Of my wavering verity. What I say in the van
Of my mind is presumption aerating into prose.
What presses my circumferences are the toes
Of my journalese in the sallow loam of pan-
Demic sense, that what I first wrote arose
From the paranatural, as if some demon chose
The void in which to cancel me. But who can
Do better than to lour verbatim of the street,
Not as humble deference but as supernal law
Which accretes into statement as a rickshaw
Of sticks to carry spines of the easy elite
On cobblestones of facts that hardly endure?
More than this is less than easy sinecure.

Still in the image of body is the shape of air
That rises afar, in eddies of the sun, as gold
Of spirit, as medallions of bronze in the fold
Of ships of the coast, where inlets are a lair
For prows that lift forward, where keels spare
Outward tumult of wake awash and white in cold
Marine that smoothed when the Holy Spirit told
Once helmsmen to sail under the rounding flare
Of seascape light. Where is the embodied Word
That walked on water in myths of eternal care?
But if it thrives, then I may languish, absurd
As I am with unholy opinion, billowing to bear
Gold templates of television though my clothes
Are rumply old, not a sail, nor petaling rose,
But empty as air.

No News

It happened, as we thought it might. The vision
Incorporate, and seldomly incorporeal, was ready,
Softly and warily geared, so immensely steady
Before a golden khan of news, but a hard elision
Swept in, away to a nil hiatus of excision,
None, nor even variegate, nor even a heady
Fail-safe feature from Soho. Beddy-beddy
Bye-bye, anchor winking into sleep's decision,
Zzz, broadcast nationally so at redundant five
PM. What a row there was and is at this,
Even juncturing when heads of state, I wis,
Were out to lunch or dozing, nor wont to strive
For any fancy upstage plethora of talk,
Imprinting, nor anything up the clock
To stitch or weave or knit or keep alive.

Television Evangelist

Unbelievably benign, he knows you, reciprocal
As you watch and listen, ameliorative and quick
To Sunday lustre. Before him, you are slick
With caret dew that twinkles. The gospel call,
Included in his sentencing that is like a shawl
For one's indenturing, is lilt of curlew settling sick
Within his pining rhetoric. Verily, the trick
Is getting a flock to be as generative. The hall
Of his knowing is his mirroring. His cause
Is everything that anyone might gestate in him
And more (the gesture and the honied hymn
That belt his vaster audience with measure),
For what he knows he knows and says is pleasure
Unto him as, wonderfully, he mouths his gauze.

Machine Press

The cast steel trundles on rollers over the floor,
Heads and gears and blocks, the instrumented
And casual weight that rumbles like war.
Subtly heaving, it turns under chains regimented
As tackle by pulleys and the spring of steel.
The machinist, in his careful scrutiny,
Shifts the weight, smoothly turns a wheel,
Pushes and glides, eventual as destiny,
Careful as God with the impress of pain,
And swings with it in the magnificent air
Because he holds it stilling there.

Then he turns to the ritual of the press
In a reverie for some mettle of devotion
And opens it, by a handle raising it less
As a matter of fear than of competent motion.
A myriad times before in the grave
Towers of precision he had judged his surety,
Had vacated chance with a wave
Of concern and rational purity,
Had, in his wisdom, wielded his fright,
Had willed what he knew until it was trite.

Then some slip of oil gleaming on the floor,
The thrust under, the jostling weight
Incalculable and wandering, and the shore
Of precision, where? His palms near the plate
Of his sacrifice, the handle and descending forge
Press his thumbs and index fingers paper thin
That will not grasp the even world again.

Seven-tenths of a Second

There's the tree, shaded and stolid as death,
And you, in the impress of speed, a mile a minute
On a register, weigh forward with your last breath
To note in a curious gravity the casual limit

Of an illusion pressing you to settle still
Forward at three thousand, two hundred pounds.
In the compression the bumper flows into the grill,
And its bits of steel slip into the tree with sounds

Of puncturing; the hood rises and waves into the shield
In front of you as the drive of wheels lifts and hovers,
Twisting openly; the grill spills its flakes, annealed
Into colors of light; the body steel covers

The trunk as if a casual mantle sloping in
And corresponding; and the rear enfolds and splays
The doors that move like tongues floating in
A discourse of the day. Your body plays

Against its speed as the structures near you
Brake you easily: your legs reach straight,
Snap at the knees, leaping short, and shear you
At the groin; off the seat, your torso like a crate

Settles into the dashboard as your chest and arm
Curve the steering wheel; you crest into the visor,
Though you cannot see the pitching motor block harm
The chipping trunk, for you keep speed, wiser

Than before without knowing; the steering column
Bends vertical, and you, driven and impaled,
Fail inwardly, pulsing blood into your solemn
Lungs. Your head is mantled and assailed

With glass. The car reclines into the ground,
Conforming noisily as hinges rip, doors pry
And rail the air, and seats rise, puff, and bound
Forward to press and pin you where you die.

Ascent from a Divider

As if hollow ground as a knife may be, the divider
On the interstate stiffens this variety's market
Of hot, rousting cars in narrow lanes like a carpet
Rousingly undulant, and my mind, like an outrider,
Divines the madness of its consistency. I fire
The atmosphere, throttling, as it exsufflicates
Gaslight carbons of petroleum and exacerbates
The slipstream glare. There, instantly, a tire
Mark on the divider, ecstatically aplomb, suggests
Parabola. How could rack and pinion put it there
But from severe angulation of chassis and frame
Across the lanes, splitting airborne, rattling fame
Of chrome, engine oil stippling through the tests
Of torque, then there, easily ascending, dissolving
Into antecedents of terror, to die forensic, revolving
In the sky, to be metalled in a Bessemer of sun?

Emergency Landing

The air stops, still before a fan
That seems to shine like a meandering tine.
Low before him sun like sun, before him glare, line
Of wire catenary, and the rising road, can-
Can tossing grain below, and the wide scan
Of power caught in louvres winking. The engine
Closes down, sputtering, to reel and whine
As winds do, downing into a fence. Tan
Light glistens, gleams into alternatives lost
In a vertigo of vertigoes. The underpinning breaks
Through, into him, splintering his weather and shakes
Wings that crumble in. Now the prepossessing cost.
He is there, in grain, astride himself and worrying,
Balance gone, astute to know, seeing, hurrying
Inwardly as before, but still.

Forsooth!

Two rings tinkle on tempered glass,
And a clerk, tempered too, will pass
Opinion hovering, for whom class

Might be high church anglican
Or paeonic Mazatlan
For purest Teotihuacan.

He know himself and, auspicious,
Looks down, lordly suspicious,
But notes, certainly, their precious

Money becoming obvious. They will buy.
They know they want rings, though why
Is nebulous and they a trifle shy.

They unfold the money to inspire
His patronage. Their love will fire
A smallish diamond that will not tire

Forever. What a slipping on
And a turning, the light upon
Her finger where, suspiring, dawn

Is. Facets hardly dimming
From her trembling, slimming
Words of troth lightly skimming,

Lightly said, but said here
Before him, a churchy, churchy mere
One demonstrative. They fear

His urge to sell to anyone, seeing
Rings around, their golden being
Round as an easy race for freeing

Love. Which ring no doubt for what,
Finger round for rounding, she caught
Them always. The two had wandered, sought

Rings here, and she, gathering
Them closer to her, feathering
Discussion, keeps them, weathering

The moment for eternity. Well,
By leaving quickly, they might dispel
The petty voyeurism of a clerkenfell.

Freeway

The curve and dip of the Santa Ana,
And across the sunstream palms gust
In their transigence. Green and rust
Of sun on roof are a scape, and sienna
Rouses from the hint of rain. Old Vienna
The music finds a rhythm in the lust
Of color here. Mounds of rock, must
Of drying trees, ochre, a bandanna
Of blue break through, light floats
Toward the sea, shadows rise and reign
Over arroyos, and the south will pane
Experience bleu and rouge as motes
Of glory linger over cities and a host
Of swallows nestling in air, the coast

Of oceanic blue bequeathing them.

Marathon

It ends, ends with an obelisk down your leg
As a sweep hand defines the rigor of time
And the penchant of feet to remain in lime
That hardens in saline. Heaving, you beg
Inwardly against triumphant will to reneg
On vision, black spots verifying your mime
Of legs and arms forwarding in the clime
Of a gauzy mind that totters like a peg
Spinning and listing in. One further devotion
Up an angle of repose on which you ravel
The wind that brought you gusting to cavil
Against theories that are less than motion
In the cause of winning: stones through the hole
That was your marrow and you in your winsome role
Before the viceroy of ultimate sleep.

The Twentieth Maine Regiment at Gettysburg

On the first, second, and third, the trident
Of the blood's Poseidon sank deeper, afresh
To the sea of its origin, and when, godsent,

It became the standard in Lincoln's flesh,
It sank again more firmly, for sallow troops
Prayed as penitents, wielding sleeve and mesh

Of arms, with bayonets, frantically in loops
Of mind, arresting and recovering to hold
A yard of rock or ground where the will droops

Only into mire and lesion.
                              A blade will mold

In time, if kept there, wet in misting sun:
The fragrant hill below, where peaches fall,
The lisp of leaves, the broken lines that run

Into ditches, the weaving and irrupting pall
Of smoke, the riband near a rose, the trickle
Of dew, the twinge of thorn, and the dying call

Of a horn. There the dull gray robe and sickle
Prevail as the finger feels a fragile spear
Of bone. Who were they of the bronze and nickel

Medals who received canister and shot at the angle,
Devoid of power that flamed the face? They railed
Into death, fumbling the flags of war that dangle

Now from stakes. Off white and dimly unassailed,
The monuments stand where the dying, once impaled
In weeds, flourish into the air of another century

As yield of new orders and in Christ are nailed
Into lengths of rhetoric that seem less than fury,
Less than insurgency, and less than incidental worry.

Hitler in the Black Forest, 1944

The flow of green is taken in the mail
Of evening unto the emerald Parsifal.
The joy of Nuremberg is the frost of fall
That melts in the touch of a sudden sail
Of light. I journey in the steel-blue pale
Of plates of air. Gently, gently the call
Of Siegfried settles like a hymn against a wall
And echoes here. A trill awakens quail
That scurry into foliage and disappear,
So taken in the hush they rustle hardly more.
I touch a vine. It trembles as I rear
And stamp, neighing, to keep the lore
Of the reich I nuzzle in. Aryan blue
Invests the oversoul that rose and flew
Into the final siege of evening: heil, heil

The End of a German Army

Summer in the Ukraine, when the grain is cut
To stubble, is access to the treadmill links
That chunk against playtoy wheels in rinks
Of motion. Sprockets find the rails they mortise
In, sinking into depths of dust as if to entice
Attention, as if to acknowledge the order and device
For victory. The sun wavers and sometimes winks
In this trespass, though sun summers in the rut
Of war. Columns wend and rollick in the practic
Row of discipline. Then Von Paulus, in a field,
Marshalls his staff, who entertain the yield
Of vast terrain to Stalingrad. See the thoracic
Demeanor now, in Moscow, shuffling as they cleave
Claret with topaz memory. Ice will sheave
These 80,000 now, and death will mull
Them standing, standing down in fields.

The Invasion of Europe at Sainte Mere Eglise

Day of crystal
             without curve or facet
                                    clair
or spiritus
             Chartres
                                    luminescent
as cool glass
             flowers tossing
                                    like wind
seacoast
             faint mist away
                                    horizon
tolling web
             larva as in a tree
                                    silence
of Sunday
             languor of light
                                    smooth green
chambered air
             wash of sand
                                    white as porcelaine
spiritus of stone
             crucifix
                                    Mother Mother
throne of Jesu
             alone
                                    aspirant

prayer
        larva still
                drone of height
arriving
        from a sun-bright sea
                the soul is sun
shaken into light
        sepulchre
                église
sanctus sanctus
        invasion
                hiatus of daffodils
crosses of stone
        against a wall
                salient of white
Ile de France
        awakening
                le coeur
claret
        rustling forward
                wind
gray ships
        against the gray
                holinesse
of sand
        mirador of blue
                washed from blue
the holinesse of war
        after die walküre
                Ghost

To a Prussian Officer (April, 1945)

Because I died for you, you need not die for me.
I am the Fisherking, who would gather you to me.
Take my hand. I show you leaves of oak and linden.
See the ochre, brown, the darker green, light hues
Of green, the rising green that passes into sky
As if to mellow blue into the radiance of green.
Green of the forest darkens far into evening
Where dusk must slowly deepen. Remember Israel
Of the flags away, for over them a falcon brandishes
The light. Here, in my hand, is the sand of Canaan.
It wends down from me, lustrous in the green.
Because I died for you, you need not die for me.
The old gods kept the faith, the very discipline
That keeps you near to me in memory. Walk with me.
You wear the uniform of the lightning of the sky.
You brace to hear me, but I am the wand that moves
Against the air. Weep now that the regiments
Stood at Nuremberg, hailing ave, Mary, Mary,
Weeping, sieg, sieg, failing as the leaves
That touch the stone and pass away. Feel the wool,
The leather of your belt, the smooth blue medals
Of the air, the tumbling steel of hands that mark
Your presence in this viaticum. Easier, now.
Rest next to me. Remember the olive tree that gnarls
The years of my remembrance. I am the father god,
The fathering of brown and green, the fabric stiff
Against your arm, the shoulders squaring for a covenant.
You are lost far north, beside the gray and sloping sea.
See the cathedral reaching into rain, the arch

Like the corner of an eye on end, and, unending,
The scape of darkness where the glasslight wavers,
Beckons inwardly. The way is dim, but a shield
Sustains the slope of evening. Silence now,
As you kneel. The arching gate of Brandenburg
Is open to clusters of your people, in Saxony,
In Prussia, in Bavaria, in the citadels of kings.
Keep the fervor and the fire gently as the Rhine
Transpires to the sea. This emblem is the iron cross
I soften into gold. Wear it in the evidence of Light.
You need not die for me because I wept for you.
Put the gun aside. Sieg, sieg heil over death,
And keep me near to you.

The Wall:
The Vietnam War Memorial
in Washington

The list goes on, in these multithousands
Of its gravure, without particular note
In a tryst with itself, on black, but to dote
On it is a duty. It is a sarcophagus. Wands
Of light pass over it, though the alien lands
They came from are near us now. Côte
D'Azur remembered, we recall or lightly note
The visions we favor, the urgent rote
Of napalm ascending. Feel the fueling sands
Of phosphor settling in, red as sunset and remote
As war. This is cold earth in perpetual stone.
But we must sense the cone of a vertigo
In the pane of any seeing, the failed imago
Of their dream caressing fire. Then names atone
For it and stay, versions of remembered being.
Wending here, we touch the cold, hardly seeing
The closing light of sun, and wisps of snow.

The Ascension of Ramses II

Amun Ra will bring us in a streak of light
And power into the sky, and in the thunder
Speak his verity. The sky trickles under
Dark clouds to envassal and lowly sunder
Gray willows of earth and river to affright

The air. The streak is the streak of under sun
That glows as fire along the clouds like tassels
Of the gold necklace I wear within vessels
Of the rain above, beyond storied trestles
Where one may pass. So we pass undone

To make arcs of the sky in our transporting
Elision. The sessions wander down and, dimming, go
Beyond tomorrow. The will of Amun Ra will come below
The tabled air, where our will is. We wait to sow
Our vision. The soul runs and rifts away, sorting

Threads before the vision and roll of thunderheads
That amass and move away like the presences
Of ancient dynasties. The minor mortal senses
Fail. But we know the leap of light, evidences
Of bursting land, the epoch of the meads

Of death in declensions of the mystery of stairs,
Leading down. However low, the spirit will rise
In the brilliance of a thrust of air. The spirit flies,
Does not, will not die, but starts awake, the prize
Of Amun Ra in the lexicon of vanishing prayers

That soul must make, that earth must make in the weirs
Of what we know, whatever lightning takes or spares
For resurrection.

Daughter of Ancient Egypt

I find the water at my fingertips.
Whence it comes is a sea of stars.
Sea to sea it moves, where vision bars
Dissolution only for a time. Time sips
The memory of my grief, and my lips
Must meet it full. Here, a faun nips
Quietness until I know it too. Jars
Will keep the kings as Sirius dips
In its azimuth. My dissolution comes
Across a winnowing, where dust arises.
It follows across my sight and devises
Solace, where the goddess hums
A threnody. Isis, attend my silence.
I am Egypt riven. I am the valence
Of your honor, dying with the sun.

Egyptian Immortality

Venusian of the crescent moon
Beyond the unseen rim and the disc
Of the gold effendi, can you risk
The tales of a sultan and the sun
Of the golden pharaoh in the noon
Of his glory? A silent whisk
Of sand shades the stone bisque
Of time. What remains is the spoon
Of aloe and the rest of the immortal.
The pharaoh nears the low dark portal
Awake, for his great sun shone
On a mask's flowing gold, the cone
Of the wind, and the river of evening
Across the sand of a delta, flowing.

The Pharaoh of Atlantis

Comparisons of sun, assisting sun, here and here
Among the myths of pharaohs, you gleam before Atridae
Of the fleece and coming history. As on heaven's tray,
Sirius, you seem citrine, afar. I dream you near,
In an effulgence, and caress a memory where I peer
Afield to see and see. Your golden light will stay
On the edge of memory's vast skiey field. I stray
Before you in inconsistency. You keep devotion and appear,
As now, calming this viaticum. There will be mosque,
Or minaret, or chapel as the gift of evening dims,
Aglow. See, your gold is here, along your azimuth.
The silence tinkles, gold on gold where a silver moth
Emboldens memory as a field of stars brims
Horizons where they appear, light on light unending
In your immortal light, in us suspending
Golden light in a finer radiance.

The Pharaoh of the First Dynasty

Can it be that the very air is burnished
To forgetfulness? But I remember
When his glory was, for he spoke, furnished
With eternal memory. The salvor of December,
When the sun shone lavender across the marsh,
Brought the median gold across our linen
And slowly closed the iris air within the harsh
Night of tombs. And now I awake in the tannin
Afternoon. The pyramids have fallen into rubble,
And I come to see the remnant of the trouble

Time has come to, in its elision. Precision
Became angles into the air, not the Nile
Of the wending. Where is the supernal decision
Of our science that was the gleam of tile,
The plaques of alabaster, rising? The incising
Is of the star, Sirius brightening near,
Of monuments. Vishnu, let your bier
Wend through galaxies. We fend for Amun Ra,
The victor still. But the tannin light we saw

In the sudden morning of Atlantis is a record,
As we know from strands that keep identity.
How old is morning in the air, the bright chord
Of our first resonance? Was it our sanctity?
See the crystals tumble from the star
And fill our eyes with wonder! The immortal blue
Holds their resonance in gold, or tannin far,

Since the very sun, now dimming, though anew
From the epoch of Atlantis, can never fail
In the syncretic gold of origin or the tale

We tell of dynasties

The Tomb of Ramses II

Look down. One's sorrow is a tear
That vanishes in the quiet air,
And Egypt's power's image is the pear-
Shaped headdress in the Pharaoh's bier.

The painted wood has been the lid
      Of that patron of the golden sun
      And his seven necklaces may so stun
With glory and array that one might bid

For a place amid his still antiquity.
      See the cartouche, the Scarabaeidae.
      See the lotus flower in eternity.
And see them each in their ubiquity.

The Pharaoh aimed his straightest arrow
      As the Falcon drew him and his kin
      Through time victoriously, not like Saladin,
Who came and vanished like a sparrow.

Lakeshore

Softly residing, waterfowl harbor the silence
That lies like patina over the water; eastering
Wings whisper into shadowy vales, sequestering
The sunset gild that silvers into dark ambience.
The aria of dayspring leaves me quiet, alone:
My hand moves into green for the glowing stem
Of a flower that tosses gold in a beam of gold
That the evening sky rendered in fading, cold
From the leewardings of air. As angel pro tem,
I marvel on the edge of the lake at the contours
Of light that assail the standing dark of night.
I move upon the light and stand in the tours
Of spirit; there beyond the closing spell of sight,
Or in vanes of feeling, I move into the light
That fins the air with lustre that the spirit stores.

Cabinets

They seem as new as turned wood at the sanding
They were put to, to achieve the smooth grain
That they reveal in the empire of the soft stain
And varnish they received. Above the landing,
They reside in shades from a light suspending
Halcyon effects of the personae that reign
In history far beyond the smoothing plane
Of any builder. And now we revise, attending
Memory with a choice of keeping blends in time.
What ladies billowed down, near the balustrade,
To meet a marshall of Waterloo to enfilade
A soldiery! Cabinets hold their finery in the thyme
That scented it, and their sachet, in memory
Of soldiers that broke an Imperial scythe of cavalry.

Cemetery

The honeysuckle lists into the eminence of shade.
Valencia and the wisteria of the western sky
Dim into a hush of color. Who is there in the pale
Of distance? Some have passed into the jade
Of cloud, into the ciel of song, into the rodomontade
Of vanishing storm, and they, committed, will not fail
Their accountancy. The petalling hues, mail
Of their presences, remind us of veneer—
The place, the remembrances, shadowy Vermeer
And tall El Greco repining when they appear
To court the lines of spiritus in the mere
Of the palette. The colors leap in the dark air
Against a certainty. The touch beyond the care
Of immediacy and the tremors of blue share
The voices of knowing. Hear the bells,
The shimmer, the skiey cells, the ciel, the wells
Of infinity together.

Alternatives

The tentative storm skims in, and thunder mills
The levels of cloud, serrating them. A cozy bay
Of hills, awash with patina of sun in the array
Of the west, offers warmth in nooks and over sills.
The intrusion wavers into silences and reveals
Where one might softly ask admission. The lay
Person, unacquainted with such antilogy, must pray
For concentration. Rumbly, one; smooth,
The other. Ten children find the paths unto
A stream that spreads diamonds in lieu
Of any sequestering. Which will soothe
The soul or mind? Freshets come from both
And train alternatives, though one is loath
To say that winter is as fine as spring.

Antarctica: The Crown of the World

The higher latitudes rise, shelving still
Higher in the storm, and ice, the overburden, will
Slip and fall, vanishing for a moment, to mill

In darkness and to reappear, divesting particulate.
The dark overwhelms the sky, and winter, late
Until now, descends in its longitude, elate

In curvatures of the world. Once, in the vessel
Of lands, the sea uprose and drove a tassel
Of light into sun that languished in a trestle

Of rain. The great wind swept on, to sough
The sea into versions of the Valkyrie, to muff
Into silences what might have been. The chuff

Of breathing, held at the lip, is the backwind
That flees into reaches of the equator, finned
With steam, like the piranha. Forward, pinned

To the sky, are sails that are rarely seen but kept
In memory. Fire enflames the wind where we slept
Before arising to fury. Beyond, in the transept

Of the seventies stirred by reaches of harder cold,
Vanes of the world purple the montage of mold
In the light of sun, if it were seen. The gray fold

Of the filtering dark is down the red wine
Of dawn. For this is equinox in the deft shine
Of the sun's declination. Higher still, in the mine

Of zero latitude, the wind thrums as if on steel,
But over the jutting stone of the apex, to anneal
Pain into the vane of weather across the vast wheel

Of revolving. For this is height, and the earth
North is deep in its comfort, wisping its dearth
Of weather, green as a forest, dull in its berth

Of Cancer. Far north down under is calm,
But winds here are forever washed in the psalm
Of winds, lissome in violence, beyond the palm

Of Mercator.

New Delhi

Four minarets seem and seem tips of blooms
That rise from a central arch that encloses air
And the distances of air, in a row, in the care
Of a Buddha whose arms stir where air resumes
Into Nirvana. This montage of effects exhumes
The silences of Atlantis, seaborne in grace, whose lair
Is Origin. The people here below must spare
Themselves that memory, for they, aware
Of need, provide interchange in rooms
Of azure for conversation for which they chair
The charismatic speakers of eternity who, fair
In their declensions of lotus, survive in tombs
Of the past. Seven for eternal seven spare
The scent of renascent heaven, where bare
Simplicity becomes a quintessence as fair
As light in mist, where luminous India
Is the sepulchre for the Buddha and the Brahma
Of history.

An Evening of Stars

The severing green, the green of forests, and the emerald
Field of the sheen of evening, so wield the vision
Of summer that the star-designing star of sapphire
Strikes down, prizing the evidence of fire-
Citrine Sirius in the radiance and precision
Of aquamarine. Colors open. The solar shield

Is gone to other suns, and they softly wield
Their light in the soft velour of Monterey.
Pearl and amethyst brim in the dust
Of galaxies beyond in the deepening dust
Of light where the Pleiades gather to pray,
And then in the afterlight play in the field
Of forever.

Exogenesis

In the ∞ beginning of the galaxy ∞ GOD created
The heaven and heavens and the infra-planetary earth.
And this such theoearth was without ovoid, and the dark
Was upon the surface of the altar void, and the spiritus
God passed over illimitable plasmic oxygen
And the organizer ∞ God said imprimatur Light,
And there is Light individular and ex cathedra
Popular, etc., e.g. here facsimile, versing us,
However (elate).

Grotto

The sea, rising toward the arch of the moon,
Surges in, amid the palmleaf surfaces of green,
Sintering its spray to singe the dark between
The orange fires of fluorescence and the plume
Of sun in shafts of amber in the watery room
Of clove, dusting ambergris. One seeks the mean
Of midnight sun where glitter is the haloxene
Of lime turning yellow in the heavy noon
Of upper sky. Down there, the coal of bluest nitre
Vales the wash of spindrift glimmering caramel
And citrine. The phantom light fulfills a dell
Of an emerald reverie. A swirl of bistre
Settles into the coral silvering to a whisper
Of starlight. Whisper, whisper in the vesper
Of moonglow under this wisteria.

Habitat

What is lost but lesser things? The rings
Of light bequeath the glow. The afternoon
Is an elixir of air. The breasting tanager
Is far afield, pecking as a manager
Of minutiae in his weeds. Too soon
For understanding, he hops, darts, and sings

In that order, affecting other birds. Robin,
Larger than before, is affecting red.
He is quizzical because another told
Him what to do. That buzzing in a fold
Of flower is not for him. Soon, well fed,
He keeps at it, switching like a bobbin.

Who told the airborne how to ply their way?
They are, in extremis, busybodies
Exacting fantasies in early summer.
But intruding early, late, a hummer,
Up from Mexico, asserts prerogatives
One cannot abide and, like Morgan le Fay,

Knits the air, hovering. What do I care,
Resplendent in my blue, sunning gold?
Certainly I enrolled myself in a fair
Of my cerulean. And why should I share
Domain? Though hardly serious, others scold
The lower denizens. But look from under where

I vanish in the rarer blue!

Inscape

See the languorous sea verging
Endlessly into form, all the quietness of supernal
Mind, glacial distillate of earth's silicate
And hydrogen, and else, never crisply desiccate
Or dusty unto death. It flows in, this blue eternal
Over the setting of concomitance and over the diatom
That glows, in the Godly soul as if in emerald wine.

Key West

(To the poet Caedmon)

Remote on the archipelago, what will keep
You reticent? The waves surround the tumult
Westering into a gulf. The idea is a disorder,
How storm plays against itself at the border
Of the sea that rises as if to inflict an insult
Rising cold and harsh enough to make one weep

From wind. There, there is order lightening
The land while lightning is sierra inveighing
Against the mulling sky that darkens gray,
Whose nigre is its slave, whose ghost is the jay
That only interrupts the rattle of the straying
Cone that finds importance here. This frightening

Exclamation after the ellipses of the keys
Becomes Key West. A fiction lies on your table
For a piece that you will languorously create
As sound. The sound must find its way, elate
To find an order. The pen dallies and finds the fable
That beckons as the sea does when it frees

Crescendo in a visitation of a mythic presence
You must define. Your sentencing is lyric
Too, as fine as ambergris and lapis lazuli.
Across the waves, where pastels must flee
In twilight's westering, whispers a panegyric,
In which the keys are implication. Immanence

Above the sea offers periods of light and sound
In the hush of a distant storm of what will be.
The present swirl of it is ecstasy, the lordly touch
That takes a phrase and keeps it not too much
For reprise, as if a Pentateuch and the key
To such magnificence that you once found

As Key West of the English period.

Sunmist and Rain

The scape surprised itself, allowing clouds
To range with skiffs of rain that aroused dust
To mist the sun. And all was changed like rust
That brightens in gentle rain. Chambered shrouds
Of evening settled across palisades amid crowds
Of leaves in sunlight. The haze was like a trust
Of holy England, whose ancient and sepulchral fust
Of Columbine might be in error here like the dowds
Of Cambridgeshire who assail customs of a habitat
With ranging supervision. But all was far west
Of Greenwich time by a quarter turn of the palimpsest
Of earth, and the heritage of romance, in bluest matte,
Stilled the memory. When were we lost in this cove
Of psyche, sometimes blown, remembering mauve
And the tapestry of kings?

The Lady of the Sound,
or Rime of the Modern Mariner

The myth of dreams and the dream of light
Are just beyond the tapestry that shades
The depth of self, the self where trades
Lift the coastal sand before the flight
Of swallows where a warming sun is white
As alabaster, where the sand of glory abrades
The lordly sky. All is hidden. Memory fades,
And it is gone. One cannot, wishing, render sight
Of the consonance and chiming. Who can indict
The list, the formal green, their regularity
In which one tells the stories that reveal the clarity
Of secret knowing? Mumble what we knew, slight
With thumbs and grimy fingers, aboriginal and trite

When we are always new.

Moro Mon

We came from the islands of the sea
Where the silver azure lies in fire
And from Jerusalem, that rests lee-
Ward of the gold and near the spire

Of light. The memory remains
Like the crest of tumult bearing
North to northern lands in stains
Of early morning, starlight faring

Away, away. The cirques attain
The song of water, hollowed high
From the rasp and curving chain
Of ice and icefall where eagles try

The mist. We have kept the saw and awl
To shape a ship again, to find
The cleft and the redstone hall
Below the cleft, back to the mind

That found us here, now aware.
For we remember the fiery fleece
That fell across the silver flare
Of vision and the templed peace

Of Solomon. All hail! The kings
And judges mark the river curving
Down from tablelands. He who brings
The conscience comes, comes unswerving.

Ritual to Romance

In that confusion the immediate coral almond,
And then in the sand the saraband that revives
The wind. What must it renew? The spirit shrives
To awaken. The evening cools, and the wavering pond
And the sound are midair, a mirage, slipping the bond
Of radiant light. It is evening, and the soul contrives
To confine its confusion and to shine in the hives
Of awareness, shimmering with worry. The wand
Does not fail, for it slips the steady wind, outreaching
Stillness. It stirs in the softness of sapphire
Across a lake as light entreats the iris fire
And imagoes of the sea. The whispering and beseeching
Is the birdcall, the whispering. Reach out there to touch
Soft radiance or down, never more and never much,
But quite enough, deep in the dark Atlantis, like the shire
Of soul in old Granada and Castile, and the isles
Of Prester John.

Seas

The sphere of seas is as limitless
As the transmutations of space and time.
Seas transpire into themselves with motions
And colors that cast themselves from sun to darkness
And reverberate up the downing synergy
And fade and fade in the skylight heavens
That suggest their variance and veneration.
Tenors play as on lyres that subtly echo
Winds: the seventies south ring the world and rise
Like a warlord beginning war, fury into fury
Rendering him. Fields of spume assail
His violence to define Tau Ceti a universe away.
Seas are the meaning. They are plateaus and plates
That assail pressures of change, flame up as colors
Of vulcan, and sinter into ash or water.
Seas flow into their specific gravities
And enact the sun.
              See, within, the glint in her eyes
At twilight as it flakes and flows with understanding
And hallows visions into glory.

Seed Crystal

Across the distances of time, time is not,
Nor distances that distend the sunning vision
Of immediacy that inspires in our derision
Of death, that footnote that provides a plot
For delusion. Reality is somehow caught
In the stress of quantum time. The revision
Of that rote becomes the very elision
Of error amid slow tinkering, and sense a blot
On history across a sequence of immortal dynasties.
The crystal of immortal remembrance falls
Into the lotus green, into lapis lazuli when the halls
Of Luxor echo with appropriate asperities.
For it is timeless in the ghostly dignity
That resumes its symmetry in a fine civility:
To know of immortality gives rise to find it.

Shades of Blue-Green

This singing green is olden style
Even for Marvell, who espoused the tropic keys
South beyond the dark Bahamas in the breeze
That, swelling, edges off the sea to while
Palms into listless waving. The tile
Of sea is Mercator's grid of warm degrees
From the golden gulf that calmly streams
Far north to pass the darkling glacial seas
Of Greenland and Iceland greening in the file
Of Northern lights and the fan of Ellesmere.
See the heavy fronds of sapphire intercept
The pale green-yellow where great Orion kept
Orange light in a galaxy, and green in the weir
Of the vacancy. Wind is green where the scape
Is ice or palm, touched cold in the shape
Of sea, green mounting into higher blue.

A *Thousand* Galaxies

The corporate view is lighter than bluebells
Arrayed in the litotes of the surrounding garden.
See that daffodil arising in the blue, the warden
Rose and the fern, the pasqueflowers, shells
Of honeysuckle across the pearls of light, and wells
Of darkness in between! How in the cordon
Of knowing them may I touch them like a Corydon
Bustling amid his flock? But some are knells
Away, light years plashing over them, extending
Genesis the invention. They gust away,
Imploring a revision of the first pretending
That became the real. See this lovely sway
Of them I give to you. They rustle over satin
Into velour and hush away like an antique matin
Of a holiness.

A Unity

Misericordia, the light falls in, burnishing
The centre. A fine propriety shapes
It round, flows into crystal, resides, and capes
The resilient fire. Imagine the furnishing!
The spirit waits for it, exigent and famishing
For the mana of its gravity. Who must traipse
Through psychiatry for the remnant, drapes
Of silver all around, to find the vanishing
Light in me? Take the centre from a nebula
And drop it in to nestle where it will.
Space depends on being. Nor raise the sill
Called intellect, no more than it, a fibula
And erector. Our history is a faith, the draw
We saunter down to find the lakeland and the law
Of our ubiquity.

The Thunderer

Indian summer basks in summer,
And its incandescence shines like porcelain
Through trees and across the redstone stain
Of the patio. Over lazy poppies a hummer
Hovers, quietly drowsing. A drummer
Seeks a hollow, red against a vane
Of brownish light. Seasons attend a chain
Of years that keep them open to a thrummer
Of a mandolin, as if he were a solitaire
Amid the changing. Each formality is a reprise
As my high storm widens and falls to seize
The rain in shafts across the grassy fair
Of the land's gentility. Weather's the ware
I sell across the visions of my modest care
In this neighborhood.

Whispering

The thrush will sing, and its echo, down
The glade, will gather softness across the ray
That is lost to evening as the wending day
Loses brilliance westerly in the down
Of whispering. But nearer then, and drawn
To secrecy, as a reminiscence, it will stray
Into itself, abounding gloriously, to shine
As if one could see it as a burnished line
Of color from the brush that brought us May.

And I have seen imperfect May address
The spirit for a time in a fine assertion,
Wondering softly how possibly a desertion
From the probable could so caress
The light. But it will come at once to press
Into being like a prayer, like an insertion
Of sapphire into a crown. The brightest day
Of song will come, itself fulfilled to pay
Its own ransom in a fine diversion.

Trans-Mississippi

The water swells near the shore where trees dip
And mask the surfaces. A boat drifts away.
A girl in it glances and performs a lay
That is soft as a murmur. Silken leaves drip
From a gust of rain. Swallows rise to knit
The air with crossing flight as they stray
Into twilight. The girl vanishes to play
Into the emerald future that must ease and tip
Into a restlessness of waves, where she must wait
In a cove of reeds for him. Together, they gather
Their belongings for the crossing. They would rather
Eddy west in the air, and will, in the strait
Of light to Denver, west to the Sierras and La Jolla
On the sea, where waves rise like passion in a Goya.

Xanadu

The vast arch of Grenada keeps the sky
Still in its repose. Its sepia merges
Brightly into blue deliquescing higher where angels vie

Into the testament of glory: light. Evening, evening surges
Softly into night, into the drama unseen but silken
Into darkling color, lower still, where an erlking urges

The sudden whirr of wings. Faeries awaken.
As if a saint, he rules the vetch, but harkens
To the whispering. What may be said, taken

As a verity? One sees the eyes. What darkens
Into pools? Who prims eastward, in a vale?
The lotus passes into darkness, where lichens

Shine from stone to stone. Ah, Psyche, hale
Amid the darkling stars of the Pleiades, hasten
From Atlantis into caesurae and the pale

Of the greater metaphysics where we chasten
Theory. The even hush of knowledge will soften
Into violet, and heaven's holy rain will moisten

Knowledge into spring.

Breakwater

The sea, far welling, is a new horizon, sill
Of distances, coming here, Poseidon revelling
With winds. Not Poseidon, but an overlord delling
Into cataclysms, roiling the dark, in rain. That hill
Of water turns as it quakes, spurges as God's will
Into the atmosphere. In it, tacit, spelling
The hover of mistletoe glowing in dwelling
Diagonals, he enflames the air in the twill
Of a hurricane. He comes into the heavy margin
And speaks a thunder. But now not he, another
Cites the mail of his existence, and he must hover
In the manger of our dream, that his chagrin
Created zephyrus, a holy breath. He rides a crest
In his claret, in his stately vestment west
Of the Sierras, as the intimation of the rest
Of what may come in the giant red of his Mars,
Cooling some.

Conquest

Generations fold away into the past.
I stand far west, along the meridian,
The bays and bayous, the obsidian
Of Seti I, the crystal cathedrals that cast
Shadows of themselves, caught at last
In memory. Remember old shadows, the pavane
Of light, the loss. And now I scan,
West of Sur, far light along the coast,
And seaward too. Prester John wandered south
As I, forming Africa and legend, find
An archipelago where distances may bind
A dream into the real. The Pharaoh kept
His stars for wandering and his dynasty as debt
To heaven. I render him in the guise
Of novae barely seen, where the heavens rise
And rise as night.

Blue Ridge

Blue, blue as mist is blue against a deep horizon
In the afterglow of the hesitant light withdrawing
Down the west, into the hush, worlds away. The sawing
Katydids arouse themselves in night's liaison
With day. Day brought the weft of day, the diapason
Of being, all passing through the settled lowing
Of cattle, abroad in the staff of light, the sowing
Of grain, and togetherness, as in the French paysan.
O country, you are here, and here, like far Lausanne,
And I collect the hush of the ambiance of light
And shadow in an Angelus in the falling view
Of sun that glistens sepia in the shining
Pale of tomorrow. Who will it bring in the sleight
Of dawn?: drawn into promise, his, his own,
His lordship is the sunburst after, after rain,
Now sparkling dew.

The I

I have come into this bayou in the barque
Of my soul. The winds stand tall
In their circumference, away. Terror, stark,

Address the air, breathless in a hesitant mall
Of calm across the gray. The clouds surround
The low horizon above the abrading squall

That folds ships into sea. I reach a sand mound,
Faring beyond the shore. I hear the sound
That I can see. I leach air and ground

Into manic evidence, steel light held or bound
As hydra sway. Fronds hang at the forest's edge,
Aglimmer with dew of starlight, loosely wound

In wreaths of verdure. Up there, the only ledge
Away is cloud or heaven. The storm breathes low,
Beyond. Starlings rustle, aware. The sedge

Is dense as theory, chastened by the flow
That went before the eye. I am the threshold
If I do not move. I must always move, low

In light, verecundiam, to regale my cold
Insouciance. Look. The rain clouds fold.
I must move, newly here, where winds scold

A verity.

Sand

The angle of repose depends on the moisture
Laden in it, but a skiff, if dry and blown,
Whisks into atmosphere where its tone
Is beige, beige in blue. Sand to lure
Attention quietly is heaviest when pure
With water. Sodden in a cellar, cool, alone,
It is lost to the very thinking that I hone
So wistfully. But sand it is that I immure
To dry, paling from vain lustre too,
As its moisture passes, warm. It can fire
To glass if pure, seen through, a skiff of blue,
A pane, so cool, though slowly flowing still.
Sand is smooth, whether wet or dry, the will

That blows away, or gathers into nooks,
Or in mounds of the Saharan perimetric
Beige, until horizons are unknown or eccentric,
What you will of heavens whose clouded brooks
Of blue ripple far away, seen, unseen as in books
Of the holy wind. We set all this out in the diametric
Universe, away, as if among the stars we may trick
Ourselves into disbelieving. But see, out there, the rooks
Of light, of sun reforming, in the granding photosphere!
Sand is of the diamond day, heavy now, or sheer,
Lifting as with wings, and flying, as they appear,
Before us, streaks winnowing and feathering,
But in this baptism of the stars the weathering
Of will, the glistering, starry tethering,

The round of this infinity of grains of sand,
Of Abraham the sequestering, the very land
That God and God's will made so near at hand!

Off Cape Horn

It is the world of its assertion where the world
Is sea, where the wind falls in a sphere of violence,
And now in the history of my lost indolence
I cheer the ship that sails the heights of furled
Light vanishing before the steel and falling cloud.
The pallor veers in distances that shroud
Opacity. See the twinkling dark in the dense
Blue weight of the sea, and the far bright sense
Of tomorrow. Tomorrow is away, pearled
In litotes. The flail of water in the evidence
Of sight dangles the mace I do not see. Near the tip
Of the mast it descends to touch it, falls to rip
A sail, and lifts across sheer latitudes. I languish
Inwardly as Antarctica disappears, and the ship,
Awash in jetsam, retains the thrust of anguish
In the diptychs of a Solomon. O overlord,
An angel falls to save it on a wave, and there,
Beyond, are Juan Fernandez of the calm and the gale
That furls north to Capricorn, where it cannot fail.

Paradise

Grave time, mirage and mirador,
You bend the light in your gravure
Of space until in space the pure
Light falls where near time is sure
But limited before the door
That opens to a brilliant room.
See them resting in the tomb,
The paladins of palisades
And porticos, where a loom
Is weft with hovering shades
Of glory: this shady knoll,
This peridot, this mistletoe,
This shadow of the moon, this plume,
This solitaire of evidence
That soon becomes the spirit's mind
In the flow of the world's asperities
Of cold and heat, as if the Word were
Less than providence or bistre
Yellow of the sun!

Crusades

I found Ara at the Auto Electric, where I had come
For his skill in repairing circuitry under the dashboard
Of my car. Perhaps he was as Armenian as the sound
Of that name, and when I learned his surname, I knew
He was, though the western land was his home. "Ektee!"
I heard, as if a bird had conveyed more than "k,
K!" at the perimeter of sound. He went to his task
As quickly as I told him the problem. Afterwards,
Coming to me, he told me that the repair would take
The day. So, as he continued, I sat in a foyer
And consigned myself to solve my schedule and return
At four. "Ektee, ektee!" the plaint rose, and I was
At once Richard Coeur de Lion of the Crusades, afield
Against the Saracens, and yet here was Ara, and I
Whispered that God had come to Armenia to call him
From the sallow fields to believe, and he did believe
In the remonstrance of spirit, as a Christian to be, now,
Though from an ancient century. Ara, stand. I place
My arm about you, welcoming you for Christ the Lord.
You have kept the generations of your Armenian name
As a sanctity, through the lists and the assailing flags
Of the Saracens, keeping faith. In our descendancy,
Armenian and English, we are west of the far Azores,
At home together, easily discussing a need I have
For you, never now thinking of the ancient divisions
Of light that kept the shade falling between us.
The old lands are a memory of man's worldly schism
In himself as he foundered through the dark abyss,
Where sailing out alone bequeathed the current danger.

Ara, stand. I shade your hand for your ancestral being
And the ancient belief in me that eventually brought us
Here for promise, where the cordillera reaches to Mexico
And high Canada, where the versions of distant flight
Encounter the still high air of the western sun
As it settles west into the dark horizons of land
And sea at twilight. Almost a birdcall, "Ektee! ektee!"—
"Come home, come home to me!" the shepherd whispers
Near the edge of a grove, as the wide river murmurs
Like a threnody.

The Undemocratic Process

The
O
demi-
Urge
to circum-
Vent
Policy
is like
Rosemary's baby.
You never know
when
it will scratch
You.

Conscience

What is this glory but the sense of tremor
At the edge of feeling, where a fountain
Plays through sun discs as the mountain
Of rivers suns the cirques? The blue tenor
Above them is the bearing blue and, then, the mirror
Of the dark in which mirrors hang like Ton
Of the clustering beyond. The sense of dawn
Over the East is suggestion, and the Knight of fervor
Is Galahad of its Order. Then coral is the chorale
Of epiphany, for it will break the sea into foam.
The white breaks in upon the plane of sand to dome
The isle of our reflection and to make it moral
In the poise of sun in which we prize the godly,
And our achievement is a heaven, here not so oddly.

Christ the Magician

Beryl exquise the lamp of level light
Or laser the impresario the castle moves
As if the cloud were still Betelgeuse.
Now of whom is whose despite
Its independence, flame the supervention
For: all else is will and his retention
Of variety, sleight, the watchful I, light
As the hand instilling.

Sherrizah

Calla lilies are the vestries of the air
That hold impression. Somewhere, spare
In visions, their white is softly fair

To keep embossing latently in white,
For if the Word arouses height
Of drowsing gold, the very sight

Of memory will play again in being,
Rousing the first creation in singing,
Vision involving, devolving, fleeing

Into the crest of space and the curve,
Inveighing against the darkness to swerve
Amid the lilies of metaphysics that serve

Its cause.

Faith

Narrow it to conviction; nor let it stay.
Pain of variety must be, be it the same,
As constancy. Across hieroglyphs lame
Insights toddle into being without the play
One might associate with artifacts. I say,
They seem a servitude of the mind that came
Along with old philosophy, that old name
For wonderful repute, trifling like a jay
Through scholarship and logic. What is older
But the ancient name none can comprehend
Of the one one cannot gainsay or easily defend?
He lives in penance like a saint to shoulder
Sinai to its destiny, whose name will not molder
In the avenues of sun, though it may be colder
Than before.

Hello

Walking intently through passages of sun,
He keeps a rare pale light around his face
As if he had decided how very well at eighty
He should be, or how immortal. I saw him
Pass into the north as if it were a transept
Of morning, where homes abide in fields
On either side of the street. He was alone,
Separated from care around the corner, east.
So I found it in myself to keep concern afresh,
Though the silence was pure as the sound in trees,
As leaves kept court, and birds were heralds of weather.
I went to the wooden bridge and looked after him
As if expecting him to rise through fallow light
Into the heights of meadowland and cirrus petals
Of cacti pale from dew. But he had turned back,
And I met him, at a distance, with an easy "hello."
He came immediately to me, with the somnolence
Of whitest white, his hair luminous as frost
In the aureate white of his belief, knowing me,
And concerns of immediate history in the fief
Of his sentences. The counters of his meaning
Feathered his intonations until what he quickly said
Was dressed for the panoply of the clouds and hill
And the vast estate of spring behind him, dazzling
The skiey daffodils across the fence and grasses
Of its verdure. He wondered how all were, here,
In the field of willows. And I saw, in his report

Of disciples, what he must leave them, even now,
Before his transpiring more fully as a persona
Of his own events. What can remain but events
That pile over each other, stone upon stone, rising
As a wall? His spirit fled in the blue-white
Wind, and wings invested the leaves, busy
With experience. The lean philosopher would know
The pillow of his presence, historian the bleak
Accoutrements of awareness and the fobs of thought
That pile forth into the conscience, constricting
The nets of what he meant: the presence increate
In the space around us, murmuring with silence—
He and I, together, he in his witness, I in mine,
Understanding the pause in silence, the diamant
Clasp, and the weave of the prism's spectrum
Passing into the presence of words.

Prophecy

Touch, at the height of glass
Overbending. Rule to pass
Into the vision of vision,

Flower of the belling light.
The feel of claret, blue height
Intermixing in the blue-bright

Bay of the spirit, infolding.
The holy seven come, withholding
The will in forgiveness and scolding

The grave. He is risen, risen,
And he is come, so riven
That glory of these seven

Circlets is the will, the flower
In the circles of the heavenly power
That comes with him as a shower

Of rain.

Sunlight

How anciently it reigns over papyrus
And waterleaf, sunlit samovar, egregious
For our destiny. I see it in a palm,
And the palm accepts its reign and balm
That smooths it, the vision of the siege
Or rush of time. Smooth in the hush,

A voice from it is magic supervening.
I care to speak, and should it flow,
The denizen of sky lets it shine
Dawn the abyss of green to refine
What is in the flow of what we know,
Collecting versions of its sheening

Mirrors mirroring the golden round
Of sun, corona wavering to heights
Of maelstrom, cones, flakes, and flares
That spill again, collecting lowly shares
Of gravity. Then in supernal flights
Creation minds the winds of sound,

A whispering.

Theology

It is a lilt against leaves where there is no form
But the constant variance in the tremor of stars,
A disquisition. And to come as less than a storm,

Warm in preternatural light, not so given, it was
The face of history in the consistory of awe.
It brackets the furnished light that is and clears

The smooth vision that is the universal law,
And then must dread a circumspection that seems complete.
Word lustre pervades the glow, and one must draw

The circle larger. Fail us longer. The seat
Of knowing is the speed of light squared
As the counterpoint of the rest. Delete

The study that is no study, for it flared
Into circumference and is largesse
Unending.

Archangel

The carriage, at the curb, tips and rights
Itself as if a shade of shadows had stepped
Up and in. Who was it? The evening kept
Its obeisance like the formal lights
Across the waters, beyond. Within them kites
Of the lower world meander where Hades slept
Before the fires of light consumed it. Who wept
In gardens before, to know of lost heights,

That upward inversion of this abyss? Gentle
Angel, Michael of the ploughshare, fleet
From the upper regions into the waving wheat

We wander in, such gold before a lintel,
We sing of you at harvest. Our shade is but a mirror
Of dusky water, ghostly in the terror
Of our transfiguration.

Bible

Then, southwesterly, the sea arose
As if the moon hung near to draw
And keep it near. The ship tipped low,
Its sail the shape of a paring,
Clearing the margent sky, where law
Is made into the yield of thunder,
Where statement is a textual wonder,
Even testament.

Atlantis

The versions of history emerge as from a cornucopia,
The array of refraction of its light in a diaphane.
Hush, hush. They exhibit themselves for the utopia

Of feeling and seeing that has been. Now from the welter
Of sea and air the insurgence comes, the reign
Before Time, at 4000 B.C., the immediate sun, the shelter.

Ah, Atlantis, the halls of light, the range of conductors wane
Into a unity! inspiritus, easy into easy being,
The range of knowing, in the pyramids that have lain

In the spirit and mind since the beginning, since seeing
Became the soul of the triumphant God. Valencia
Or Venice was never as strange! Down from the fleeing

Night-winging stars, the swallows of unity, O gracia!
Hover and stay. Mercury, swift, swiftness, the tone,
And there are paradigms of Osiris, lapis lazuli, lucia

Brilliant in water! The melior pauses askance, alone
As the height of the centre! Gales of the energies
Pale in the Venusian stream. Where dark planets shone

In reflection, the pylons rise, and from a lea liturgies
Come. O Egypt, you are now, Khufu of the gleam, tarmac
Of the downwind blue.

Brahmin

Fair lotus, sun of green green in a pond,
You rise through levels of our existence
Into the matchless union of suns and the prescience
Of the Taj Mahal as it wavers like a wand
Before the veneration of wind chimes in the fond
Clime of our mortal hours. The moth, intense
As Vishnu and Brahma for the penitence
Of the Valkyrie, revises the horizon's blond
Twilight of morning and evening. Lotus,
You float in forgetfulness. Dust drifts away
In the clarity of silences. What can a Brahmin say
Whose doctrine, now wending, rose and smote us
With reality? All, all is reflection in water.
For all that is, the wavering, what can I barter?

Christian Martyrs of the Renaissance

Fond giver, the lustre of your giving
Is a sacrament. It grew from thorn
And thicket into sacrifice, but is worn
In vision like the honor of our living
Before the cruciform. Here now the hiving
Lords of an inquisition convene, forsworn
In their own eminence, but they are born
To history as brackets of venue, contriving
Place and honor in their niches, where marble
Shows them evocative and, in legend, statuatory,
Therefore doubtlessly and dubiously hortatory.
The dim hall of halls holloes their treble
As we walk. Their dust has settled, strewn
In cloister and in memory. A far, far tune
Of a whippoorwill is our will in this consistory
Of our presence as we wear away their history.
Gems may be dew, dew from the inspired breath
Of feeling the humble words one saith
In our devotions.

Ethos

Bless the word as it appears as evidence
Of what is, should be, might have been.
And how does it summarily appear when,
In accountancy, it is the experience
And closure of the good in the prurience
Of sullenness? Cross the vasty fen
Of thane Macbeth that inspires the sen-
Soria and esoteric diffidence
Of the self-appointed righteous awe
Of O upstanding and imposing Law.
None may conform, for form is a flake
Of snow with its blessing, the white
Of endless supererogation, not the spite
For ways of thinking, but a way to slake
A thirst beside still waters in the wake
Of a mission, without closure, without flaw,
But on the tongue, like the mind's Excalibur.

Evening Storm

The clouds trim themselves, billowing low
To cover the lands with rustling nigre. The charming
Rite of evening fails wherein the west, disarming
The rise of sleep, settles golden over a row
Of hills. Far in the clerestory height the flow
Of wind is susceptible to stars, where his farming
Is a glow below the sickling pharaoh who, alarming
The night with the verity of Indus, might show
The antecedent will of the sunning creator
Who pales the nigre with strewn dust of the praetor
Who affirms celestial glory: Rigel of the blow
Of the diamond wind, tumbling bright into power,
And Betelgeuse blown into red and the shower
Of fire in the bower of Christ, the sower
Of grain in the fields sinking lower and lower
Now to touch the earth with the lyre of beginning.

Faery History

The continuous hieroglyphs are like a stitch
That plays out when the thread is drawn.
Time pulls that thread as the pharaoh, wan
In his desire, extends it. The consonant pitch
Of eternity is the faint monotone I catch
At the sound's edge of light in a lyric dawn
As whippoorwills discuss the weather. I don
That cause. Sean, the playwright, wrote a batch
Of plays that will occupy a golden niche
In the tomb of the early Celts whose green Christ
Was a faery intimacy of soul. The pharaoh's tryst
Amid his artifacts and fetishes provides a lich
Wake for the Christ, enlivens eternal history,
And Erin, Egypt, all attend a faery consistory
That brings them forever home to Him.

Malory

I shall not blend into the sea
To mist the purple strand; I keep
The strange before my eyes, for I sleep
Near the strand before I doze to see
The images God brings me before I free
Them across the page, before I leap
Into the romance of princes in a heap
Of books. Were they mine! I flee
From old restraints like a bird in a hall,
From door to room and out again to fall
Into the azure cloud. Knights may call,
As an echo might to Arthur, to enthrall
This kingdom in a mystery. A library
Kept in Egypt keeps me too, a February
Flourishing into spring, books in an array
Of my remembering the King I shape to stay
In the legend of my lore, which, when done,
Is more: Atlantis from the shore
That is the full corona of the sun
That glistens Amun Ra to endure
The eras that blend before the King
At Bethlehem.

Intimations of the Holy Grail

The green seems fallow, even brown, in the dim
Hollows of forest, and Geoffrey, lost, redeeming,
    Restores the providence of dreaming,
    What to furnish, and what to limn

As legend in the gesture of the pen.
Years will soften as brimming years elide
    The list of facts where lichens reside
    And soften years into the wonder of a ken

Of stories from the Maenads of the lake.
How is it, then, that King Arthur rose
    From the place where poets doze
    To create a kingdom for their sake,

In Camelot? If once the Grail appeared,
It was enough to furnish me with scenes
    Of knights with shields. The lady keens
    The legend that, unfulfilled and feared,

Was less than faith. Merlin rose from shadows,
Dressed in his dreams of shadows too,
    And as the very lightest do,
    Sang remembrances of the meadows

Where kings could come, where the Savior's story
Could be told in the magic of a miracle,
    Where life became the lyrical,
    As if the King might sing his history

In psalms. What measure may be fairly taken
If not the fair? The fair for everyone
    Is the memory of palisades that sun
    Themselves in the glow, unforsaken

In the spirit's realm. The spirit furnishes
Its own desire and brings it into being
    As Galahad and Lancelot, seeing
    Honor, come with lances. Who burnishes

The crests I see? Knight errantry
Is evidence of him, of that belief
    That is gentle as the lightest leaf
    That graces wind.

The Last Supper

I am the wind of sky and cobalt. In the gravity
Of my seeing you, you possess yourselves in a civility
That only you can muster. Your fine servility

Foreshortens you or restricts your discipleship
Amid the quasars of my power when you lip
The knowledge of the integer and slip

Into a sleep of faith. My hand swirls
Across the galaxy as its claret brims and purls
Into a stream of stars. Whose intent curls

Into a faith of silver? Rise, Johannes,
The field is hovering in light. You press
Near me like a century bestowing a caress

Of time. The meridian intends the final cup
That I must hold. Rest in me as you sup
The clarity of light. See, it trembles up

The winnowing of stars. Ah, the windrow
Power yields, in me, the windward flow
Of testament, and I must hear the rooster crow

Its limit at the touch of a day to come. Rest
Before my spar and mast; the enduring test
Comes before the eye of the pyramid. My behest

Is in you, though you squander drifting regions
Of your awe. The hollow years house legions
Of your children. Charlemagne, your pigeons

Rise like sound to signal home! Europe rails
Through wars to see me hold the light, but sails
Of testament will open full. Who wills

Them so but Him? Pray, now, as you touch
My hand. Is it now, too soon, too much
For you to see me rise where you must be?

Limitation

The penchant to include the stars
Is born of mind, since it wanders
In deltas of suns. God renders
The illimitable universe, but chars
Creation with the drifting cars
Of bluelight fire aswarm from embers
Slipping far away. Then cinders
Float in the stillness like avatars
Of Satan to touch the voyager
And pierce him through. The escarpment
Of far horizons withholds us diffident,
No matter what the false excalibur
We might brandish. Feel the seizure
That makes us aspen, even evident,
Constructed fragilely as a feather
In any sort of fiery weather.

The Other Mary

I am the shade of a leaf that moves in light,
Sunleaf, greenleaf passing near. I kneel.
I take his sandals. I feel him touch
The hair across my eyes, but not so much
As to shade my seeing him. Birdflight, birdsong
Keep me near the wondrous sun, whose warmth
Is dayspring through. Now I bring his sandals
To him that he wore in Galilee.

Prophet

The future past, past the vertigo
Of striving, attrition gone, turn I
Inward turning, come and go, try
The me of my flickering imago,
Tell, impressing imprimatur of why,
Assailing, sailing, blown, for my
Insilvering, asea.

Resurrection

I breathe the upper air. My circlet flame
Wisps into it. Magenta and violet flame dark
And vanish. The rose of indigo, lost fame

Of Indus, aspires into the crest of this stark
Evening in the apparition of the Zion
Of my spirit above the sunning barque.

I deliquesce into crystal as the scion
Of the Elohim, ave of Virgo paling
Into clusters of novae and the failing ion

Of their origin. Skies will be the tailing
Of my fire in the argon of the faith
For which I am the principle trailing

The sophistries of doctrine. I am a wraith
Astream in galaxies. I invest the cause
Of my nativity. And I am and saith

The universal aye.

The Rhetoric

Gently, gently exude, into Oleaceae, vowels
Of Cicero as glacial proof of lanolin,
Then, moreover, old-time Senecan in TV's din
Of fricatives and ball peen. Steamy towels
Slip veils of silk or isin-flakes of stone.
Soft rondeaux spiral into light to convey
A May of rhetoric. However, don't, per se,
Count on them for more than the basic tone
Of the Baptist or the Beloved. See the foal
Of language as it totters forth in innocence.
It is holy before such hard experience
As rises from expedience across a shoal
As wave. Christus, impresario of the sepulchre,
Hush our vocative of power across a burr,
The genuine.

The Star of India

The high mast spar tips with the wind
Aswarm with the drifting sea rising
From the lash of wind. The suddenly arising
Sun is gold patina, though sometimes I find
Finned ebon in the sea. Twined and twinned,
A sundog filters sunset air in the isin
Of light lost and open beyond the sizing
Nearly mind. Fall of sunburst white and finned
Outrides the versions of plateaus beyond the eau
Of vanishing. The Star of India rolls in
And lifts, as if hawsering the din
Of crest and foam. And now I know
That sailoring before the mast is far
Into the agency of knowing light and spar
The Crux of heaven.

Sun Hero

The first light, in its consonance, sprang
From itself and filled the concourse of space,
Inventing and investing itself in a trace
Of circular motion, swirl of verity that rang
To be! Now, evenly, it billows like silk
In air, and light years wavering through the grace
Of gravities, through the strait and the place
Of holiness. The lyre is here, where the milk
And honey of Canaan are origin in the solace
Of forever, those billions of light years as a trace
Of thinnest light, but there still extending!
This is his only belief, arousing and impending,
Never vanishing, and isotropic, as Rilke
Knew. Song of his Self will traverse
What is and never is, becoming the universe,
Transfixing, though slow, Thou defining
In Thou transfusing.

Angels of the Abyss

Into the sepulchre of frozen flame
The stretch of blue wraps the silver green,
And one is taken up as if the coral reign
Of the reef could hold sea against it in the name
Of the under-Poseidon who burns in the sheen
Of darkness, down. The gulf is the main
Sector, whose waters permeate the marine
Of atmosphere that gills the wafers of fish
And urchins posing in their preeminence
Of flashing gold and gray and wisps of fin
Finely decorative. These angels wish
A plebescite at the final bar and the experience
Of swifting light as it is known
In the red shift far away, when it is wine.

Archaeological Find

The line of metallic gray vanishes into the shore.
The high bank there gathers solemn darkness
Where moss hangs and lichens nestle in the caress
Of decay. The heavy ages decline into the lore
Of reversion. Behind me, the sun may restore
The height of air into the prism and the stress
Of memory. Buildings are as pieces of chess
Awaiting mind. Dull gold in the store
Of past events will maintain its even lustre
Into another age. The layer of ozone is gone,
The sun at noon defies the earth, and the tawny
Lands embrown and char. That fuming bistre
Fans its fire, soft as a waning lumen
Amid the galaxy, where these men or women
Lie fused and interdicted together.

Telepathy

What one needs is proof that it exists.
We know of the tangents of psyche that bend
And bond to accommode the lumens that spend
Themselves along and in, as it persists:
Telepathy: that is, it is. A tension wrists
Once over, excitable, apprehensive, to wend
Still further in just out of reach, to fend
Off a doubt. Its rhetoric is sinuous, lists
Of grammar for it in the mind you know,
Yet it is so expedient. Take the telephone
In hand, dial, and hear it ring in the zone
Of your knowing that it will or will not sow
The psyche, receive or not receive an answer,
Especially when it wills, out there to incur
The aspen desolation: a telephone alone
And jingling for response, no, no tone,
And the chasm dark, no, nothing, and the burr
Of silence there, and here, tele, tele, weir
Of nothing, and this absolute the O and mere
Of desolation.

The Closing Iris of Escape, A.D. 2531

Since the storm of methane over the char
And ice, I have kept our records as I do now.
Once vision was of the heavens, what mind will allow,
Horizon to horizon the fullest aperture, the quick car
Of our transport in the illimitable hush, far
Light of the sun a twinkle in nigre, how
We see to return to the blue pale of the Thou
Of our kept religion. This, then, is the mar
Of our plan, the spheroid weight of a zero.
We might have returned, and yet may, or not,
But the heavens are now the ever placid night,
Strangely an iris closing, improbably wrought
In desire and guess. The once irruption, slight
As we felt it, tilted us into an impossible lie,
To an angle badly and lowly depressed. The dry

Cold absorbs our last power as a needle reads
Down into loss. The iris of meaning scans
Subtly to array our science. The white fans
Of dust still overhead. Very soon, someone pleads
In a murmur, breathless. This, simply, among needs:
Only a chance to return. The commander nods, as he plans
The touch of Greenwich time, and lists, when he spans
Trajectory, to peer into space. Too slow, in the weeds
Of our sorrow, too low to return to the higher curve
That may bring us in. Even so, we will softly glide
Down and away, lost in unavailing silence, to swerve
Into gravities of light, away into the loss we deride
With tongues of our silence the incalculable disaster
Of accidence through distances we never could master.

A *Change of Venue*

If one knows the jack of daws,
He might know the king of cause.
Newton, after appling,
Took up the art of dappling
Theories with doubt
Before Einstein indubitably
Turned the curve of space-time inside out.

Glacier

Late snow is early now, now over autumn.
A patina of snow lifts to drift, to assail
The curve that forms the cirque, to pale
The borne snow of the col. The veriest drum
Of skiey platinum tines the thinnest hum
Of the quasar sun in the hyaline. The vale
Of sky above the bowl, silver over shale
And rock and precipice, ends as I come
To this height to know the timbrel metronome.
The lost azimuth bequeaths the dark wisp
Of its eternity and the Word in the lisp
Of this geology. Strata formed from seas
Of the ancient world, to remain a reprise
Of my knowing myself in this frailty.

The Higher Science

How can firelight burn? Only if the mind
Does, turning substance into energy in faith,
The hypocrite fury renouncing the inner wraith
Of flame that makes mind bright in a wisp of wind.
How can silence sound the timbrel wish or the kind
Gesture of a bluebell shaking? The thinking rind
Is cortex, bole, and what man is, he saith,
And what he saith, he affirmeth, layeth
For himself as antique store. I speak Christianly,
Signifying that he is a thorough creature
Of himself, not in reasoning, but of the vixenly
Adoration of what he is. Let him feature
Something more, this faith, but more, ambitious
As an angel levitant and speaking gossamer.

$INRI = mc^\infty$, or Limits

Born in the prism, exhale the void of aether.
You are here. Elevate the host, the replicate wafer.
What was the whisper of history, the safer
Way to utter the word *cataclysm*? Either
Fact or exegesis will breathe it. We shiver
In red heat as the sun expands. I just as lief
Find a domain beyond the sun in the far relief
Of shadows. Uranus, you are that sliver
Of gray exponentially far, in the deep vale
Of the voyager where we cannot go. The tale
That we might go beyond is the curtain drawn
Across the lost distance of space. It is wan
Science, ill with heavy numbers. We fail
At the edge, except for the formula: INRI
Equals mc in our infinite range as we sigh
The only testament.

Another Universe

In the constant   presence the integer space is   presence
The cacophony in silken space   space   the wandering
The Venusian mitre   the mirador   the rendering.
The cambering   the ring   the ring   the Renaissance
Envisioning vast Stonehenge   the plaisance
Of ancient time   embossing presences   the Mandarin
Metonomy—we strive for these in the severance
Of the metaphysics of another realm where luciferin
Flickers out, and the gem   the Sun of waves   the Sun
Pervades the litotes of force inhering in the light
Rangeless   playing out the limitless equation   of Pi
As ought the aught of knowing   the relative mirror
Inveighing against the spinning integer   the unity
Of field that escapes its own horizon   tight
In the galaxy in the will that is or is not vanity:
The sanity the will, holding vastly in the paradigm.

Intelligence

The versions of immanence surprise what one receives
In light. And other images befriend the inner vale.
The lexicon contains a word's extension, each the braille
For another reading, each a cyclical that retrieves
A record. Once a hand fled against the leaves
Of autumn, took a color from clay and, against a pale
Wall, traced a reality in a soul as if to rail
In some language against the loss of memory. Sheaves
Of testimony allude to this, from the Origin.
Careful, now: you draw a line to touch a quasar.
It does not twinkle. Atmosphere is rare
In this immortal, and redundancy can fare
As well as Ramses did. And nothing can jar
It away, for awareness is more than mortal,
An evocation near the Origin, at the very portal.

Mountains

Whom do they abash, these wrinkles in a plate
That seem to move as clouds, and do as earth
Turns east to satisfy, as a prayer does for worth
Of this obeisance. See them mounding elate
As clouds, large and plain as they await
The resolutions of the sun, in the dearth
Of its final power, as wisps in the hearth
Of elements. They in their majesty are a trait
Of sun, a promise of the vale of amethyst
Amid the stars, a remnant of the primal
Energy, O Alpha, in a vagary of the sunstream
Will. The vacant night may hide the lists
Of their accounting, nor can the evil, dismal
In its lost gravity, pretend. They, what they deem,
Restore a grandeur that is not lost in dearth,
Atoning light in light, the upward col of white,
Arcturus in the vale of clouds, the dust, the earth
That floats away in circles of its relevance.

Seyfert

So incredibly dim, thinnest disc, the last
That can be seen before it vanishes to the edge
Of the universe, galaxy without arms to hedge
The conception that they exist in the distant past
Of billions of light years, you must cast
All adrift here in this tiny security of the mast
Light of Orion that drifts away too. Our fast
Identity loses form in the mire of this caste
Of galaxies of the Local Group. We have sent
To know the extent of our hours and find them
Trifling in a pocket of dim luminosity at the hem
Of Magellanic clouds in the dying scant
Fusions of larger suns. One serves the pent
Imagination as a penitente rent
As a rag and tattered as a wisp of mind
In the keys off the larger archipelago.

The Unified Field

An endless line cast to a curve in the pearling dark
Allows the universal light. They, wending together,
Found and are divinity. All turning is eternity, stark
Vacuum of nothing but the echo or the gusting heather
Of energy. There, beyond, is the mind's fine tether
That we cannot drop abroad in a meadow where a lark
Rises to warble and trill. We cast our linear wishing
Along the imperial curve, but straighten it to fit
Lines of the parallax whose points are the nearby sun
Of our envisioning. If the two become one, swishing
The void and starring it, they are the endless One,
Infinitesimally then drawn into the infinite heat,
The circling Alpha and Omega, the decimal One.

Proton Déjà-vu

Itsy-bitsy, teensy-weensy thing of eft,
You suddenly sundered into sun to exploit
The void with heat, burgeoning maladroit
Into everything that is, atomically bereft
Of chemical declination and then weft
Into chemistries of your waterleaf, not left
To languish but to whirr like a quoit
Of spheres magnificently into the heft
Of nebulae, galaxies, supra into quasars
Off, way off, ultimate into the thule
Of nothingness that is something too
(All is or is not, is, however He might strew
Antimatter nowhere), taking this as a rule,
That your inflation will rebound as spars
Glinting into you, into the lesser school
In you, the infinitesimal smalling into a pool
Of you sans space and time, worming into nothing,
Gone.

The Watch

On an edge they sit forward, prim, attentive,
Listening to an echo that may arrive,
Watching the flung stars and nebulae drive
The darkness into unending time, where novae hive
To sequester power. And now they are retentive,

Having imagined all of it, even the talon
Of thought that all was one, then, in turning,
The purling dissimulation and the dark burning
Inside, like a core. So they sit, as if learning
What they mildly know. They know the pylon

Of divisive power in powers four that render
Fusion more and more. Salient versions compress
The gravities into mirrors that may redress
Insurgencies of thought that are less, though less
And less of unity. The evidence is a gender

Of E, the symmetry isolable and alone, the integer.
Their candor is their silence, though they peep
Unto themselves in tercets, for they cannot leap
A parsec nearer to what they see. What they seek
As nearer knowledge is a theory, theory to immure

As comfort. Albert, Robert, Ramses II,
Teller in the wings, ride the azimuth.
See the dusky wings arise. The moth,
Far distant, feels the supernovae fail. I am loath
To tell you more. You elicit the view

From Alpha Centauri, the edge of an arm
Of the tiny galaxy of our intimation, harm
Not here, or war, but tinkling like a charm

Of astrophysics.

Soupçon

If one should go far enough, thirty-five billion
Light years waning, one may, just may, reach
The end of space and time and quizzically leach
Slight experience to find himself in a bouillon
Of stars quite confused. But, even so, a mullion
Will expose yet another brilliant awe. So preach
Of it holistically. Kneel at Ovin's Stone; beseech
The maker. Nothing purls like fact. Apollyon,
In his dressage, invests the shapeless void.
But nothing is limitless advantage, like time
That ticks away amid these accents for a rime
That fades like blue and calming twilight, azuring
Across a vacant sky. So be now taken, ovoid
And finite, unlimited by fact that devolves
From the skiey incidence of truth, dissolving
One's limiting volition.